Therapeutically Parenting Teenagers with Developmental Trauma

Andy Fleming

DEDICATION

I would like to dedicate this book to all the carers who have opened up their family to children and young people who need a safe, secure, and nurturing environment.

About the Author

Andrew Fleming was born in Surrey in 1961 as the youngest of four children. His family relocated to Barnsley when he was 18 months old, and this is where he has lived for the majority of his life.

After graduating from a Catholic secondary school, he worked in a coal mine for thirteen years. Following the closure of the mine, he returned to education and acquired a professional qualification in working with children and young people from Leeds Beckett University. Andrew then became a full-time youth worker in Hertfordshire before returning to Barnsley to work for the local authority in a similar role. After years of running a wide variety of youth projects, he was promoted to the senior management team.

In 2003, he was awarded the Public Servant of the Year award from the Deputy Prime Minister's Office in recognition of his innovative work with young people. He was subsequently recruited as a neighbourhood renewal advisor for the central government. Throughout this period, Andrew continued to study, and he finally gained a master's degree in leading services for children and young people.

When holidaying with his family in Thailand, Andrew often volunteered to teach English at local schools and temples. Having thoroughly enjoyed the experience, he resolved to study for a Teaching English to Speakers of Other Languages (TESOL) qualification, which he earned from Trinity College London on successful completion of the course.

At the age of fifty, he relocated to Thailand, and there he developed and ran an English language tutor school that was a phenomenal success, with over 550 students studying there over a period of four years. He also became an Expert Advisor to the Udon Thani Provincial Government for teaching English as a second language. However, in 2015, Andrew decided to sell the school and return to the UK with his family to spend more time with his grandchildren.

Once back in the UK, the family decided to become a fostering family. Since being registered as foster carers in 2015, they have been fostering young people with complex needs.

Andrew regularly facilitates training for foster carers and professionals from a wide range of disciplines. He has also coordinated and facilitated a number of support groups for carers. He is committed to trauma-informed practice and has incorporated his experience in youth work to complement his therapeutic parenting approach.

In his spare time, he is an active member of his local crown green bowling club. He has been participating in the sport for only the last two years, and last year, he wrote a book called *The Inner Game of Crown Green Bowling*, which is now available on Amazon.

Table of Contents

Section 2:
TRAINING YOURSELF TO
BE A THERAPEUTIC PARENT

Section 3:
PARENTING YOUR TEENAGERS

Section 4:
TAKING CARE OF YOURSELF

INTRODUCTION

Having worked with young people in a variety of settings for the past three decades and served as a foster carer for the past six years, I decided to write a book with the aim of exploring how to parent teenagers who have experienced abuse and neglect. This book advocates for parenting from a trauma-informed perspective. It includes some theory, but ultimately, it is informed by my experience of working with such youngsters. I personally believe that an understanding of the theory behind the practice is essential, for how can one evaluate their practice otherwise? The strategies outlined in this book were born out of daily life in a house with three teenage girls, a dog and an exceptionally nurturing partner, and they have been developed over the course of many years.

This book explores the interventions and approaches that can be applied to support teenagers living with developmental trauma. It advocates a therapeutic parenting approach underpinned by the utilisation and development of emotional intelligence. It is divided into five distinct sections.

Section One concentrates on exploring developmental trauma and adverse childhood experiences (ACEs) in detail and how they inform the behaviours you will see on a daily basis from the teenager in your care. Different parenting approaches have been explored: A comparison has been made between four traditional parenting styles and a trauma-informed method, often referred to as therapeutic parenting. This approach was developed by Dan Hughes, and it utilises playfulness, acceptance, curiosity and empathy (PACE). Each parenting approach will be analysed with regard to parenting teenagers living with developmental trauma.

Section Two focuses on the parents and how they can train themselves in therapeutic parenting. This involves training one's mind through the process of creative visualisation coupled with positive affirmations. I have also talked about setting goals related to parenting. The key aspect of this section is that it explores the benefits of emotional intelligence not only for you but also for your teenagers, thereby helping them build resilience. Most of you have been parented using traditional methods and, more than likely, applied the same when raising your own children. While being trained for my fostering role, I came across the term 'therapeutic thinking', which led to my reading several books on the topic, specifically those on therapeutic parenting. This approach of parenting is different, and it takes a trauma-informed position. There is lots of evidence that it works exceptionally well with children and young people who have experienced ACEs. Having researched the approach in great depth, my partner and I resolved to try and undertake this style of parenting with our foster daughters. However, my experience soon made me realise that changing one's parenting methods is not as easy as flicking a switch. Therefore, after a lot of reflection, I arrived at the conclusion that I would have to retrain my mind to be able to react differently when faced with challenging situations. What I aimed to achieve was to therapeutically parent, in the here and now, without having to give it much thought. I wanted to follow therapeutic parenting unconsciously rather than having to consciously try to do so. My previous experience showed me that, without concerted effort or training, I would find myself slipping back into my old style of parenting. Reading a theory is a lot easier than putting it into practice, especially when parenting traumatised teenagers. Thus, in this book, I share how I trained my mind to not only think therapeutically but also act.

Section Three is all about how you can therapeutically parent your teenager. There is a discussion on how to support your children and young people in building resilience. Family life and the daily challenges you face with your teenager due to their developmental trauma have also been explored in depth, and potential strategies for tackling the challenges are discussed in this section. Communicating with a traumatised teenager, which is never easy, is also a part of this section. Developing and managing friendships, not only outside the home but also via social media, is often extremely difficult for teenagers, so it will be beneficial to look at how you can support them and help them manage friendships in general. There is a specific chapter on education and the challenges it gives rise to. It focuses not only on how you can support your teenager in their learning but also on giving them the tools to enable them to navigate a school day. As parents, you can often find yourselves having to defend them for clashing with the school's behavioural policies. Strategies that make this process more manageable are presented in this section.

Section Four is all about taking care of yourself. It talks about compassion fatigue and how the teenagers in your care seem to be immensely skilled at not only identifying your 'red flags' but also 'triggering' them on a regular basis. It emphasises the need for and importance of self-care, for you cannot develop and maintain a caring relationship with anyone if you cannot learn to care for yourself.

I describe how to work with professionals using a relationship-based practice model underpinned by emotional intelligence. We should never underestimate the benefit of sharing responsibility within a child-centred family-minded approach that aims to repair damaged attachments and the effects of adverse childhood experiences. The book concludes with a summary of each chapter, enabling you to use it as a quick reference guide as and when required. I do hope you find the book both informative and enjoyable. Remember, following a therapeutic approach most of the time is an amazing achievement and will be so beneficial for the young people in your care.

This book is for all those who care for teenagers, regardless of whether they are birth parents, grandparents, foster carers, adoptive parents, kinship carers or any other legal guardians. Since all these roles rely on parenting skills, in this book I will use the terms 'parenting' and/or 'caregivers' as catch-all phrases.

There are a series of black-and-white images throughout the book; none of them are connected to my fostering role or the young people we have cared for. The images have all been bought from an Internet-based stock picture provider. I have always loved black-and-white photography, and I did actually spend a year or more developing my own images in my homemade darkroom. I find black-and-white photographs powerful and thought provoking. I have included them in the book with the hope of enabling you to engage more with the text.

SECTION ONE:

PARENTING

Chapter 1:

WHY OUR TEENAGERS ACT THE WAY THEY DO

The earliest years of a child's life provide experiences that are crucial to their development in later life and their ability to form close, personal relationships. Therefore, when children experience warm, sensitive and responsive parenting, they start developing trust in others and positive expectations about future relationships. This is known as secure attachment (Golding, 2008). Securely attached children approach the world with confidence, and when they find themselves in situations that are worrying or alarming, they will tackle them effectively or seek help from others (Bowlby, 1998).

When attachment relationships are insecure, unavailable or frightening, a child develops an insecure attachment. Often, when the attachment figure is insensitive, neglectful, abusive or rejecting, children may feel that they cannot rely on the parent to make them feel safe and/or secure. Their development will be disorganised, and they will be dysregulated.

Bowlby (1998) identified that through their early attachments and experiences, children learn not only about themselves but also about how others are likely to respond. This learning leads to the development of a memory template for how relationships work. He called this the internal working model. This is then played out through a series of attachment-based behaviours. This means that their behaviours, emotions and cognitive processes are likely to be impulsive and non-reflective, often leaning towards the extremes of either rigidity or chaos (Hughes, 2012).

Impacts of Abuse and Neglect

A considerable number of well-documented studies have shown that a child who has experienced neglect and abuse is likely to develop significant behavioural and emotional problems. These problems can lead to a child or young person being diagnosed with a wide range of disorders. Youngsters who have a history of abuse and neglect will eventually go on to have attachment disorganisation, which is a risk factor for mental illness in adolescence and adulthood. Their emotional and behavioural difficulties will result in them being unable to develop organised attachment patterns with past or future caregivers. There is now a consensus among those working in the field of trauma that children and young people who regularly experience abuse and neglect in their relationship with their primary caregivers develop trauma, which has serious, long-lasting consequences. This trauma leads to their displaying a set of characteristics that remain with them throughout childhood and follow them into adulthood. These characteristics and traits are often referred to as developmental trauma. These traits are usually found in children and young people who have had to be removed from their primary caregivers and placed with other families and/or carers due to their adverse childhood experiences (ACEs) (Watson, 2018).

Adverse Childhood Experiences

Adverse childhood experiences (ACEs) include physical and emotional abuse, neglect, caregiver's mental illness and household violence among other things. The more

ACEs a child experiences, the more likely they are to suffer from heart disease, diabetes, poor academic achievement, or substance abuse later in life. Experiencing many ACEs can cause what is known as toxic stress, which is the excessive activation of the stress response system. It can lead to long-lasting wear and tear of the body and brain. The physical effects of toxic stress can be compared to those of revving a car engine for days or weeks at a time (Centre on the Developing Child at Harvard University, 2018).

Teenagers who experienced ACEs go on to develop trauma. They are referred to as teenagers with developmental trauma, as the trauma does have a significant impact on their brain development. Prior to further exploring this topic and trauma-informed behaviours, it will be beneficial to explore teenage brain development.

The Brain

Teenagers, Trauma and the Brain

The brain dictates all human behaviours – from automatic ones like breathing to voluntary ones like singing along to a favourite song. Therefore, to understand teenagers, we need to have a basic knowledge of the changes that take place in the human brain during adolescence; this is because these changes will have a major influence on teenagers' behaviours and emotions.

In adolescence, the brain undergoes significant changes that affect a teenager's understanding of their self and the world around them. As teenagers move into adulthood, they face increased independence, more intimate relationships, challenging and significant decisions and other major life transitions. The brain tries to prepare for this through the following processes:

HOW STRESS AFFECTS THE BODY

BRAIN
Difficulty concentrating, anxiety, depression, irritability, mood, mind fog

CARDIOVASCULAR
higher cholesterol, high blood pressure, increased risk of heart attack and stroke

JOINTS AND MUSCLES
increased inflammation, tension, aches and pains, muscle tightness

IMMUNE SYSTEM
decreased immune function, lowered immune defenses, increased risk of becoming ill, increase in recovery time

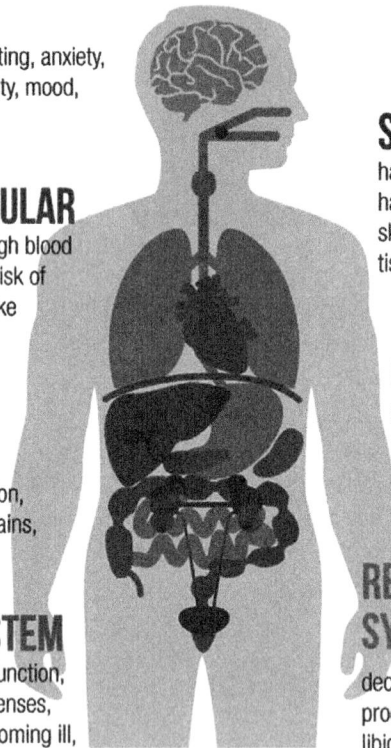

SKIN
hair loss, dull/brittle hair, brittle nails, dry skin, acne, delayed tissue repair

GUT
nutrient absorption, diarrhea, constipation, indigestion, bloating, pain and discomfort

REPRODUCTIVE SYSTEM
decreased hormone production, decrease in libido, increase in PMS symptoms

Centre on the Developing Child Harvard University 2018

Therapeutically Parenting Teenagers with Developmental Trauma

Development of New Cells

The adolescent brain develops many new cells in preparation for adulthood, which gives the brain the opportunity to develop new skills. However, without the right amount of stimulation, care, understanding and support from an adult, the cells will remain unused and will, therefore, deteriorate. There will be opportunities to develop new skills in the future; however, due to the absence of these cells, the process will take longer.

Communication Between Different Parts of the Brain

In order to feel, think and multitask, the brain needs to facilitate communication between its different parts. To enhance this process, the adolescent brain produces a coating called myelin to speed up communication within the brain. The production of the mood-enhancing hormone called serotonin is slowed down to facilitate the production of myelin. This is why you often see irritability and mood swings in teenagers.

Development of the Prefrontal Cortex

The prefrontal cortex undergoes a massive period of growth during adolescence.

This part of the brain is responsible for the following:

- Impulse control
- Decision-making
- Problem solving
- Organisation
- Prioritising
- Controlling inappropriate behaviours
- Empathy

While the prefrontal cortex is developing, the emotional part of the brain takes over. This part of the brain is called the amygdala. This means that many of the interactions that teenagers have are interpreted emotionally rather than rationally.

These biological changes take place in all adolescents regardless of their background. However, neglect, abuse, trauma, transitions and other previous experiences or environments do impact how the brain develops during this period of change. Throughout this period, recognisable behaviours are recalled. The frequently used parts of the brain are also called upon to control the strengthening and weakening of certain areas of the brain.

As part of gaining more independence, our teenagers become able to seek out and devise their own strategies for having their needs met. These strategies do start to 'shape' and change the brain. The teenager learns to develop the behaviours that are necessary for acquiring a certain response and/or having a specific need met. For example, when a child feels hungry, the brain concentrates on what must be done to get the next meal. The related parts of the brain then become stronger.

Developmental Trauma

Likewise, when children face repetitive trauma, their brain develops behaviours to help them survive. This often results in the brain being on constant alert, looking out for dangers. This eventually alters and shapes the brain: The parts responsible for fear and anxiety are strengthened and grow, while the parts that control rational and critical thinking diminish in power. The conflict between these two parts of the brain can cause flashbacks and difficulties in understanding or identifying emotional responses.

This results in the neural pathways associated with fear being constantly activated, which, in turn, leads to the brain developing lasting memories and a change in perception. Therefore, even when the teenager is safe, the strategy for surviving traumatic experiences remains ready to be used. This will make the teenager react unexpectedly and uncontrollably to specific triggers and/or the understanding of consequences. Challenging and problematic teenage behaviours are the product of the brain's attempts at fulfilling their needs. The brain of a traumatised teenager connects certain sounds, sights, smells, facial expressions, activities and body language to previous traumatic experiences. These are all stimuli that trigger an emotional/behavioural response. This can often be misinterpreted as the teenager simply 'acting out', which is not the case (see section below – What is trauma-informed behaviour?).

You need to recognise that a teenager's brain development is often affected by early abuse or neglect, trauma, frequent foster care moves and/or the lack of a secure attachment figure. The way a teenager acts socially, emotionally and cognitively may be out of sync with their chronological age. They will struggle with the development and maintenance of relationships, which will lead to patterns of intense unstable relationships. Their performance at school and home will be affected by poor memory and low cognition. They will be ahead in some areas of expected development but well behind those of their age in others.

Regardless of whether a teenager has experienced trauma, the changes in their brain chemistry and structure will feel different and extremely challenging. However, teenagers who experienced trauma must not only adjust to the typical changes but also cope with the developmental effects of past experiences. Trauma and adolescence work together to interfere with the teenager's sense of self and how they think others see them. This can be overcome in time, but it depends on the rebuilding of connections and building of new pathways (Libertin, 2019).

What is Trauma-informed Behaviour?

Many of the behaviours you see and identify in your teenagers are fear-based responses that depend on how their brains developed. Their behaviour will make them seem rude, defiant and extremely ignorant and make us think that they have anger issues. Once you acknowledge that your teenager experienced trauma at an early age and that this has impacted their brain development, you can start making sense of their behaviours and engage with what is behind the behaviour rather than the behaviour itself.

Hypervigilance

Children who experienced constant trauma from their parents focus exclusively on keeping themselves safe within their internal environment. They constantly monitor the parents for any indications of their being angry or upset about any specific situation. They are also very aware of their own behaviours to ensure that they are not doing anything upsetting that is likely to lead to further abuse or neglect. Even when they are removed from the home where the abuse and neglect took place, they will retain the need to be hypervigilant. They maintain this vigilance even in external environments such as school. This obviously impacts their learning and educational attainment. Hypervigilance also negatively affects their personal and social development for they have no time to reflect on daily life experiences. They are so occupied with monitoring individuals and their surroundings that they have little time to focus on their own feelings, aspirations, plans and memories. They are totally absorbed in keeping themselves safe. An example of this is when teenagers join a different family – they constantly observe other individuals' behaviours and what makes everyone happy. They then mirror those behaviours and formulate the same preferences and opinions as a means of keeping themselves safe. The teenagers think that they must never allow themselves to feel vulnerable as it can lead to a feeling of weakness, which increases the risk of being hurt physically and/or emotionally.

Emotional Regulation

Children who experience a secure attachment learn how to regulate their emotions and expressions, whereas children who are traumatised by abuse and neglect often express rage rather than anger, terror rather than fear and utter despair rather than sadness. It is also extremely difficult for them to regulate positive emotions. Examples of these emotions are joy and love, which frequently cause anxiety in a traumatised child. Younger children mostly struggle with a surprise day out, Christmas and/or birthdays. Teenagers generally act as if they do not care about special occasions and behave indifferently. However, what really happens in such moments is that they struggle emotionally and find the situation exceedingly challenging. Christmas can be an especially difficult time as it accentuates their feelings of loss and separation from their own family. As for love and joy, they often do not feel worthy of giving or receiving these emotions and find the whole concept of love very strange, relating it to the behaviours of a previous abuser.

Regulating the emotion of fear is exceptionally challenging, and the behaviour of a teenager who experienced trauma can escalate in a matter of seconds. An example of this could be the time when a caregiver reminds a teenager of a previously agreed-upon boundary. The teenager may feel that the boundary is unfair and start experiencing a surge in the emotion of anger. In seconds, the feeling of anger turns into sheer rage. This is due to the prefrontal cortex being engaged in the process of development, which allows the emotional part of the brain (amygdala) to be more dominant. The amygdala sends signals to release stress hormones, which activate fight or flight responses. These responses often manifest through behaviours such as slamming doors, shouting abuse, trashing their room, absconding or causing physical harm to others or themselves.

Other emotions are usually controlled by the teenager's inner working model of not being good enough and/or feeling worthless. Traumatised teenagers often struggle in accepting praise for it makes them feel anxious. Likewise, the emotions of joy and love can also initiate feelings of anxiety, which then evolve into their displaying certain behaviours fuelled by their inner working model. A good example of this is when teenagers start feeling settled in a family, lower their guard and begin investing in the caregivers emotionally. They then begin feeling unworthy of the warm feelings this generates and are likely to try to 'push' the caregivers away. To take control of their feelings, they feel the need to reject the caregivers before they reject them. Teenagers will often go through a process of constantly testing their caregivers for they do not trust what they say or cannot fathom out their motives. The processes of control and trust are all based on keeping themselves safe.

Trust Issues

Teenagers who are raised not being able to trust their primary caregivers to keep them safe and free from harm find it extremely hard to trust anyone, including new carers, social workers, teachers, professionals from other disciplines and even friends. Many teenagers who are raised in the care system can have numerous different placements by the time they reach the age of fifteen. Not only do teenagers mistrust what they are told but they often think that others have ulterior motives. The lack of trust is not only directed towards others but is also a part of their own internal working model; they do not feel good about themselves or worthy of being trusted by others. Trust is an immensely powerful feeling; if you have constantly been let down throughout your life, why would you ever trust anyone? Many teenagers who have experienced adverse childhood experiences feel that they can never trust anyone one hundred percent, and why would they?

The Need for Control

Quite often, teenagers who have developmental trauma use control as a way of keeping themselves safe. This is particularly apparent when they are struggling emotionally. The behaviour often presents itself in different forms, such as trying to parent other foster children, friends, and even their caregivers. Other controlling behaviours may include holding on to the TV remote and not letting anyone else access it, excessively moving objects around the home and denying that it was them, completely ignoring rules and boundaries, being exceptionally picky about food, and using delay tactics to make family members late for engagements. Some of these behaviours may seem like petty, everyday teenage behaviour. However, I am talking about the compulsion behind these behaviours. Teenagers feel the need to be in control as it makes them feel powerful, and they feel that this increases their level of survival. Control is a fear-based behaviour, and teenagers try to demonstrate that they do not trust the adults or other individuals in their lives to keep them safe. Food control and certain eating habits can also be attempts at regaining control because many teenagers who are part of the care system feel that they are treated differently from their peers, for example, they have to get permission from their social worker to stop by at a friend's, may only be allowed limited Internet usage and be required to meet regularly with their social worker. Controlling what they eat enables them to get some sense of control back. However, this form of control can also become the basis of eating disorders, so it does need to be monitored carefully.

Empathy and Remorse

Generally, when we talk about empathy, it is in relation to showing empathy to young children and teenagers experiencing developmental trauma. As parents, we try to develop empathy in our children for it is a good skill to have; I will touch on this more when we explore emotional intelligence in part three of the book.

It is important to understand that teenagers who have experienced trauma find it exceedingly difficult to show empathy – they probably did not have many opportunities to learn it from adults. Due to their past ACEs, they are likely to shut down their own feelings as a way of coping. This has an impact on their ability to develop empathy. Building empathy requires other basic skills such as controlling one's own feelings and behaviours (self-regulation) and naming and identifying others' feelings. For teenagers who have experienced trauma, the necessary skills of self-regulation and identifying emotions in others are affected, which means that they are unable to learn the skill of empathy. However, once they are in a safe environment and around adults who model empathy, they can work on developing the required basic skills which underpin empathy. Many carers shared with me that they had seen the children and young people in their care develop the skill of empathy. This was a significant developmental milestone that was achieved through the carers' efforts to model empathy, work around the young person's self-regulation and support them in naming emotions in themselves and others.

Remorse is another feeling that traumatised children and teenagers often struggle with. It is a complicated emotion. If you have never felt safe and are constantly hypervigilant, watching everything around you, why would you ever take time out to start accessing the feeling of remorse? Remorse can and does develop alongside empathy. However, your teenager can react to situations and experiences by developing feelings of shame and guilt, which are quite different from remorse, but it is easy to see how both emotions are connected.

Shame and Guilt

Shame is a part of children's development and can be healthy in the right context. An example of this is when parents have to say 'no' to children to prevent them from hurting themselves. The toddlers see this as something negative, start thinking that they are bad and feel ashamed. They withdraw and even try to hide. When parents see this reaction, they immediately reconnect with their children and comfort them, explaining that it is not they who are bad but the behaviour. Thus, the parents can repair their relationships by soothing their children. On the other hand, shame is quite different in the context of abuse and neglect. The sense of shame that develops from experiences of complex trauma rapidly becomes central to a young person's identity. This feeling can be and is often all consuming. Teenagers will do anything to try and avoid shame. They often employ the following behaviours: lying, denying, absconding and even trying to break the placement. The only way we can help traumatised teenagers is by changing their behaviours and working with their sense of shame.

Craving Sweet or Sugary Food

Teenagers who experienced ACEs have high levels of the primary stress hormone known as cortisol. This can impact blood pressure, disrupt sleep, negatively affect mood and reduce energy. The hormone reacts to stressful situations, and when the level remains high, it often leads to the teenager being fidgety and on edge and craving sweet substances like fizzy drinks and chocolate. Carers have shared with me on numerous occasions how the children and young people who had joined their families would always overindulge in chocolate and other sweets.

Thus, the carers had to support the teenagers in managing this compulsion without taking away their sense of control.

Living in the Here and Now

Teenagers who experienced trauma often act on impulse and live in the here and now. This can also result in a lack of focus on the consequences of their actions, which can make them act without thinking. You can frequently see this described as a 'lack of cause and effect'. Children and young people who had a secure upbringing usually do not want to undertake certain actions or behaviours; they know that such actions will more than likely leave them feeling ashamed or get them in trouble. Teenagers who experienced trauma neither have the capacity nor the wish to think ahead. Due to their internal working model, they can only see negative outcomes when they think about what is next. They often lack dreams and aspirations.

Internal Working Model

So far, I have mentioned the internal working model on a few separate occasions. I outlined how abuse, neglect and trauma develop children/teenagers' internal working models in such a way that they do not feel good enough or worthy of good things, including love and affection. However, the internal working model is more than just these deep-rooted feelings; it is more complex. It is embedded in the unconscious as well as the conscious. Without consciously knowing or understanding why, traumatised teenagers often levitate towards friends and other families that are remarkably like the ones they were removed from. A good friend once said to me that if a traumatised young person is placed in a secondary school containing over two thousand pupils at eight-thirty in a morning, they will seek out a young person with the same background and upbringing as themselves by lunchtime. He likened this to the child having an inbuilt antenna in their head that

Therapeutically Parenting Teenagers with Developmental Trauma

gives out regular signals to similar individuals with trauma-informed brains.

Biological Issues

A traumatised teenager is likely to manifest basic psychological problems. These can include sleep deprivation, bedwetting, dieting or having extreme reactions to pain, i.e., feeling no sensation of pain and/or overreacting to the slightest of injuries. They may also have issues with their body temperature; some teenagers may not feel cold or may constantly feel hot. Trauma and stress often lead to physical symptoms and/or illnesses.

Conclusion

After briefly outlining the attachment theory and the effects of trauma on teenagers, I explored how adverse childhood experiences (ACEs) can impact the development of the brain. I acknowledged that the brain undergoes some fundamental changes when young people move into adolescence; teenagers who have experienced trauma need to not only adapt to these typical changes but also deal with the developmental effects of the past abuse and neglect. Trauma and adolescence work together to interfere with teenagers' sense of self and how they think others see them. I recognised that when a child experiences repetitive trauma, their brain develops certain behaviours to survive. This affects how the teenager acts socially, emotionally and cognitively. Finally, I explored a wide range of trauma-informed behaviours in this chapter.

Chapter 2:

WHY STANDARDISED PARENTING IS NOT THE ANSWER

For the last five decades, psychologists have been interested in how parenting affects child development. But finding the actual cause-and-effect links between specific parental actions and their impacts on the children/ teenagers' behaviour is no easy task: Children raised in dramatically different environments can grow up to have similar personalities, whereas children who were raised in the same environment and experienced the same parenting can grow up to have quite different personalities. There are many other factors in the process of socialisation that impact child development. Despite all these challenges, there is a belief and understanding amongst researchers that parenting styles and their effects on children do influence and carry over into adult behaviour.

Psychologist Diana Baumrind (1967) identified three parenting styles based on a set of dimensions: warmth and nurturing, disciplinary strategies, communication styles and expectations of maturity and control. She argued that most parents display one of three different parenting styles.

Later research undertaken by Maccoby and Martin (1983) suggested the addition of a fourth parenting style.

The four parenting styles are as follows:

Authoritarian Parenting Style

The authoritarian parent is one who merges low levels of warmth with high levels of control. Authoritarian parents employ a strict discipline style with high expectations, limited flexibility and rigid rules underpinned by harsh punishments, which often leaves children wondering what they did wrong. There is no explanation for these rules. If asked to explain, the parent might simply reply, 'Because I said so'. Such parents have high demands and expectations and are not very responsive to their children. They provide little guidance and direction about potential options for the future. Research has shown that excessive parental control can make a child develop anxiety due to lack of opportunities for developing autonomy through independent exploration.

Authoritative Parenting Style

Like authoritarian parents, authoritative parents set rules and guidelines that they expect their children to follow, but they are more responsive and willing to listen to questions and negotiate as and when appropriate. They, too, have high expectations from their children, but they also provide warmth and support. When children fail to meet their expectations, these parents are more nurturing and forgiving rather than punishing. Overall, this parenting style is more democratic. Authoritative parents who use a child-centred disciplinary approach and verbal reasoning coupled with explanations tend to raise children who develop skills such as independence, self-control, self-regulation, maturity, high levels of moral reasoning and assertiveness.

Permissive Parenting Style

Permissive parents make very few demands of their children. As they have relatively low expectations of maturity and self-control, they rarely discipline their children. In a sense, they are more responsive than demanding. Parents following this style tend to be very loving and nurturing, often taking on the status of a friend more than that of a parent. They are non-traditional and lenient, do not expect mature behaviour, provide space for considerable self-regulation, and avoid confrontation, allowing their children to solve problems with minimal guidance or direction. Permissive parenting has been linked to the development of overbearing, dependent, reckless behaviour in children. Such children tend to have low levels of self-control and achievement and fail to learn conscientiousness and emotional control.

Uninvolved Parenting Style

The uninvolved parents merge low levels of warmth and low levels of control, and they do not employ any discipline style. There is little communication between the parents and children. Parents fulfil the children's basic needs but offer no support and/or nurturing, remaining detached from their lives. Guidance, rules, support and structure are non-existent. In extreme cases, such parents reject and neglect the needs of their children. Children are often given excessive amounts of freedom, which can lead to their getting into serious situations before reaching adolescence. The uninvolved parents' being neither demanding nor responsive often leads to behavioural problems and/or depression in children. Further, adolescents who are subjected to uninvolved parenting practices often feel that they have been rejected and tend to display more aggressive, reckless, hostile behaviours and attention problems.

Prior to exploring parenting methods that will support teenagers with developmental trauma, it is beneficial to spend a little time understanding the impact of the four parenting styles on securely attached teenagers. In the following paragraphs, I explain why I feel that 'standard parenting' is not the answer when working with teenagers living with trauma. My argument is that, quite often, the 'standard' approach that works with teenagers who have a secure attachment can and does have the opposite effect on traumatised teenagers.

The Impact of Parenting Styles on Securely Attached Teenagers

Researchers have extensively explored the impact of each parenting style on the developmental outcomes of a child. Here is a short summary of their findings:

The authoritarian parenting style generally results in children who are obedient and proficient, but such children rank lower in happiness, social competence and self-esteem.

The authoritative parenting style tends to result in children who are happy, capable and successful. They are more likely to comply with their parents' requests. Also, because the parents provide clear and concise explanations of the rules they set, the children are much more likely to internalise these lessons. Rather than simply follow the rules out of fear of punishment (as may be the case with children who have authoritarian parents), the children of authoritative parents are able to see why the rules exist, understand that they are fair and acceptable, and strive to follow these rules to meet their own internalised sense of what is right and wrong.

Permissive parenting often results in children who rank low in happiness and self-regulation. These children are more likely to experience problems with authority and tend to perform poorly in school.

Uninvolved parenting style ranks lowest across all life domains. The children subjected to this style tend to lack self-control, have low self-esteem, and are less competent than their peers.

Limitations of Parenting Styles Research

Links between parenting styles and children's behaviours are based on research on the connections between two or more people, but this research cannot establish definitive cause-and-effect relationships. While there is evidence that a particular parenting style is linked to a certain pattern of behaviour, other important variables such as culture, the teenager's temperament, the teenager's perceptions of parental treatment, and social influences also play an important role in determining behaviour. As mentioned, cultural factors also impact parenting styles and child outcomes. Authoritative parenting is consistently linked with positive outcomes in European-American families but is not related to improved school performance among African-American or Asian-American youngsters, who perform better under an authoritative parenting style due to their culture.

I found this both interesting and informative; while undertaking this research and writing this section on parenting styles, the information I came across caused me to reflect on how I was parented and what parenting style I adopted when raising my children. More importantly, it made me properly understand why teenagers with developmental trauma are not able to respond positively to any of the above parenting styles due to their trauma and how this impacts their brain development.

Why Does Standard Parenting Not Work for Teenagers with Developmental Trauma?

To answer this question, it is helpful to explore each of the four parenting styles individually in relation to their potential impact on teenagers with developmental trauma.

The authoritarian parenting approach is not appropriate for any teenager or child who has developmental trauma due to ACEs. The approach is immensely controlling and reliant on non-negotiable rules; failure to abide by the rules results in strict punishments, which are more often than not unrelated to the actual rule that was broken. This is immensely confusing for teenagers with developmental trauma as they are unable to make the necessary connections to understand the rules. Consider this example: A teen stays out past curfew, not fully realising that doing so will lead to being grounded (despite the parent having constantly repeated this rule). Consequently, when grounded, the teenager feels scared, angry and confused. This is processed as a threat to their safety due to past experiences and the resultant development of the brain. Unable to articulate these intense emotions, the teenager reacts by being verbally aggressive, which leads to the parent also reacting with anger. Thus, any previous headway made in the relationship is lost, and the teenager feels increased shame, which reinforces their internal working model that they are bad and do not deserve what other teenagers have. If the consequence is not related to the rule, teenagers cannot make sense of the punishment as they cannot link cause and effect. An excessive number of rules increases, rather than decreases, the level of anxiety in a teenager with developmental trauma. Boundaries are exceptionally important for traumatised teenagers, as are routines, for they help reduce the chances of anxiety and fear leading to dysregulation. However, boundaries should not be mistaken for having too many stringent rules.

The authoritative parenting style offers warmth and support but also sets high expectations. Setting high expectations for a traumatised teenager can be equal to setting them up for failure; it can also leave them feeling inadequate. This then reinforces their negative internal working model that they are neither good at anything nor worthy of achieving good things. The authoritative parenting style often involves the parent sitting a teenager down for lengthy conversations to explore certain behaviours and asking the question 'why'. This can be a good approach when parenting teenagers who had and still have good secure attachments. However, this approach would not be effective for teenagers with developmental trauma. Asking 'why' just causes more fear for it is highly unlikely that they do not know why they acted the way they did. When the parent/carer continues to ask more questions, the anxiety levels in the teenagers rise, and this could lead to them dysregulating. Dysregulation, often referred to as emotional dysregulation, is the inability to manage emotional responses. Teenagers may also consider being questioned as the parent not understanding their behaviour, and this will then be interpreted as the parent not having the ability or the understanding of the need to keep them safe. Long, drawn-out conversations often lead to a traumatised teenager agreeing with everything just to keep the adult happy, for a happy adult means that the child doesn't have to worry about being harmed. Although the authoritative parenting style can foster independence, self-control, self-regulation, maturity, high levels of moral reasoning and assertiveness in teenagers with secure attachments, it can and does have the opposite effect on teenagers with developmental trauma for it reinforces their negative internal working model. This style has scope for nurturing and forgiving rather than punishing, which does have a positive outcome for a traumatised teenager, but it would be too challenging for them to manage.

Permissive parenting, at first glance, seems to advocate acceptance of the teenagers as they are. The parents/carers have low expectations of maturity and/or self-control. Discipline is kept to a minimum. This is coupled with lots of nurturing. However, there are very few boundaries, little structure and a lack of support for enabling a traumatised teenager to self-regulate and/or lack of guidance when the teenager is struggling. As a result, teenagers with developmental trauma become exceptionally anxious and live in a state of constant fear, which leads to hypervigilance. This leaves them with extraordinarily little time for anything else and affects their learning. The idea of a parent/carer figure being a friend is fine for a securely attached teenager if there are clear boundaries. However, this could be disturbing for an insecurely attached teenager for they need someone who can keep them safe at all costs and remains calm and in control of any potential problems the teenager faces.

The uninvolved parenting style, if applied to a teenager with developmental trauma, would have no benefits whatsoever. Parents employing this style offer no support or nurturing and virtually leave teenagers to their own devices. In extreme cases, this results in a child being neglected. Therefore, a child who was removed from a harmful situation would be just going from one such environment to another. The anxiety and fear levels in the child would not change, so the trauma would remain the same. At its extreme, this type of parenting can result in the child being removed from the family. It is also likely to aggravate certain behaviours and result in teenagers who cannot regulate their emotions being constantly dysregulated.

Conclusion

Why does standard parenting not work for teenagers with developmental trauma? The answer is that all four of the parenting styles are problematic. Yes, one can see how the authoritative parenting style does have many benefits and enable a securely attached teenager to thrive. However, in the parenting of an insecure, unattached teenager with developmental trauma, all the four standard parenting styles, some more than others, are likely to cause fear and evoke more shame.

Taking all the above points into consideration leads us to another question: How do you parent a teenager with developmental trauma? We previously acknowledged that their brain undergoes fundamental changes in adolescence and that apart from these typical changes, they have to deal with the developmental effects of past abuse and neglect.

Therefore, what is required is a parenting style that is trauma informed and has enhanced therapeutic responses, one that aims to make the teenager feel safe and fosters good relationships between the parent/carer figure and the teenager. Therapeutic parenting has these qualities, and it employs a totally different approach from the four parenting styles discussed. Rather than responding to the chronological age of the child, therapeutic parenting recognises that the teenager's behaviour is often a form of communication, a way of expressing fear. This style is not about shaming a child but, instead, nurturing and making connections with an aim of healing past trauma and making the child feel safe. Therapeutic parents do not need a degree in psychology; they just need to be committed to building strong, nurturing relationships that involve strong, clear boundaries and routines and lots of empathy and natural consequences.

Accordingly, the next chapter explores what therapeutic parenting is in depth. Following this, Section Two of the book will solely focus on how parents can train themselves to follow a therapeutic approach.

Chapter 3:

THERAPEUTIC PARENTING

Many resources are available for those who want to learn about therapeutic parenting. These can be found on the Internet and YouTube and, of course, in a large catalogue of books. I have read several of these books and found them both informative and extremely useful. I specifically enjoyed the books written by Dan Hughes, Sarah Naish, Kim Golding, Daniel Siegel, Kate Cairns, Jonathan Baylin and Louise Bombèr, all of which are referenced at the end of this chapter. Further, many other websites and journal articles have contributed to the discussion. Therefore, most of the explanations about therapeutic parenting within this chapter have been heavily influenced by all the above-mentioned authors, practitioners and material. I will be adding some of my own ideas and approaches later in the book; this section is about 'packaging' all the above literature into a synopsis to explain what therapeutic parenting is – this is, in a sense, a short literature review of therapeutic parenting. Below are a set of factors that underpin the therapeutic parenting approach.

Routines

A core component of therapeutic parenting involves setting clear and concise routines for the teenager you are parenting. You need to do this to make them feel safe and secure. It enables them to get used to a regular routine without any unwanted surprises, which means that they do not have to worry about what is going to happen next. This will hopefully lower the need for their hypervigilance, making them feel more relaxed. In practice, this means having the same mealtimes and bedtimes, showering or bathing at the same times, every family member having their own place at the dining table and, for the first few years probably, visiting the same supermarkets and the same places on days out. Some parents write some of the routines on a chart for younger children and even teenagers, whereas others have them in the family welcome book as a way of helping teenagers adapt to their new surroundings. This does seem very rigid and not teenager friendly. However, having a strict routine will make teenagers start feeling safer and more secure.

Another important factor, which was also raised in previous chapters, is how routines can help with control issues. When teenagers join your family, it is important to set routines and certain expectations within the home, for example, putting dirty washing in the linen basket, drying the bathroom floor after use, cleaning the toothpaste out of the sink after cleaning teeth and generally cleaning up after themselves. These routines/expectations getting broken is often a clear indication that the teenagers are struggling emotionally and finding it difficult to regulate. This usually results in their exhibiting controlling behaviours – when they feel unsafe and insecure, they feel the need to start controlling everything around them as a way to stay safe. Examples of this can be the teenager not wanting to sit at the table and eat with the family and insisting that they want to eat in their room. They may stop cleaning up after themselves and are likely to get angry when asked about it. This can be considered typical teenager behaviour, but in a traumatised teenager, it can also be a form of communication. We need to focus not on the behaviour but on what they are trying to communicate.

Consistent Boundaries

Clear boundaries are part of the structure that traumatised teenagers need for these enable them to fully understand what your expectations are as parents. This can be challenging for you need to do this in such a way that you do not further increase their feelings of shame.

Your being reliable and consistent makes your teenagers feel safe and secure. The consistency part is especially important as failure to maintain your consistency can and does give the teenagers mixed messages, which can then trigger memories of past experiences of when they were not able to rely on what their birth parents told them. This ultimately becomes another trigger for fear and anxiety.

Teenagers will push boundaries, and this is often seen as a positive developmental stage for securely attached teenagers. However, for teenagers with developmental trauma, this is more of a test about you keeping them safe. If you give in to them by relaxing the boundary, they will interpret it as you being just like all the other adults who had let them down and not been able to keep them safe. This can be difficult and challenging as teenagers can be relentless in challenging the boundary both in practice and verbally. They also test you to see if you will eventually reject them or become angry and aggressive in your behaviour. What is required is a clear and firm response. Do not get into long debates and/or negotiations; you need to ensure that you are empathetic and that 'no' means 'no'. However, make sure that you address the behaviour and not the person when communicating with teenagers with developmental trauma. Years ago, when I managed local youth centres, I often had to deal with teenagers at the door whose actions could potentially put other young people in danger. I expressed to them that I wanted each of them, as persons, to come in, but I could not allow the behaviour they were exhibiting through the door. If they were prepared to leave the behaviour outside, they were more than welcome into the centre.

Teenagers can learn a lot from living in an environment with clear, concise boundaries, not only regarding their own behaviours and emotional regulation but also about their own personal boundaries. Personal boundaries help us protect ourselves and define what belongs to us and what belongs to someone else. They are part of one's identity and are especially important to an individual for they often define our differences. In a sense, a boundary belongs to you and to no one else. Quite often, it is a parent's role to help develop healthy boundaries within children as they start the journey through adolescence.

Personal boundaries are especially important for teenagers living with developmental trauma for they will challenge the negative opinions teenagers have about themselves. Due to their internal working model, the teenagers in our care will often feel that they do not deserve to be respected or valued. Many traumatised teenagers have had to experience a continual breach of their own personal space and emotional and intellectual boundaries. Setting clear boundaries during recovery from trauma is a way to combat the intense and overwhelming feelings of low self-worth and insecurities. The few boundaries they had as a child were likely broken well before they reached adolescence. This must obviously have impacted how their brain developed.

When supporting any teenager through trauma, and especially with regard to healthy personal boundaries, the first step is to make them feel safe again. I have related behavioural and personal boundaries together for they are both interconnected. A good approach for developing healthy boundaries is for the parent to start developing resilience within the teenager. This will be explored in Section Three of this book.

Natural/Logical Consequences

Teenagers who live with trauma quite often feel invisible and think that they have no or extraordinarily little impact on the world. Their early lives are so unstable that they never know what will come next. All this affects their brain development, and as mentioned in earlier chapters, they struggle to link cause to effect. The best way to show our teenagers that they are visible and that what they do does have an impact on the world is to enable them to understand that our actions do have consequences in life. You do this by setting natural consequences when your teenager breaks the boundaries you have set, which mostly happens due to the lack of cause-and-effect thinking. To help set new pathways in the brain that will enable your teenager to understand cause and effect, you must set natural, logical consequences. Unrelated consequences such as taking away teenagers' phones because they come in late do not help them link cause and effect. All unrelated consequences will do is cause unnecessary conflict between you and the teenager while reinforcing their internal working model and a shameful feeling that they were not worthy of the phone in the first place. Natural consequences need to be logical and applied with nurturing.

In therapeutic parenting, natural consequences are consequences that usually occur without parental influence in response to a behaviour. For example, if a teenager decides to stay up late on a school night, the natural consequence is tiredness the next day. Or, if teenagers go out without a coat on when it is raining, they will get wet. If a child breaches a boundary set by the parent, the parent needs to set a natural consequence. When applying natural consequences, I like to use the three Rs by Jane Nelson (2012): Ensure that the consequence is **related** to the behaviour. All consequences need to be **respectful** to the teenager and not involve shame or blame. It is also important not to over-punish a child, so always make sure that the natural consequence is **reasonable**. Sometimes, it is not always easy to find a natural consequence; at times like these, I have a discussion with the young person and agree on a consequence that is not only as close as possible to the behaviour but also one that both parties find agreeable.

Empathy is an important part of natural consequences. Many teenagers who experienced trauma manifest basic psychological problems as part of their brain development. One example of this could be that they do not feel the cold. It could be really cold outside, but the teenager in your care might refuse to wear a coat. Rather than think, 'Well, the natural consequence is that they will eventually feel very cold', you could try and negotiate so that they put a coat in their bag. However, if they do not do so, you could take a spare coat in the car. Once they feel the cold and its impact, you can use the opportunity to link cause and effect and then give them the coat as a way of nurturing. Another factor to take into consideration is that all behaviour is a means of communication. In some instances, our teenagers act in a certain way for they are struggling emotionally, and this leads to them misbehaving. I would never send a child in this situation to their room; on the contrary, I would make sure to put something in place to keep them close as a way of reducing their fear and/or anxiety.

Experience has taught me a few lessons over the years regarding the setting of natural consequences. Before setting any consequence, you should always take a minute to step back to avoid acting on anger and/or disappointment. I recommend that you go through the process of using the three Rs. Once you identify the appropriate consequence and are confident that it is connected to the inappropriate behaviour, apply it immediately. Once the consequence is set, you should enforce it, as failure to do so gives the teenager mixed messages and makes them feel that they cannot trust the adult to keep them safe. Setting the consequence ensures that the teenager links the cause and effect. You should never overpraise, but do acknowledge a young person's good behaviour. Overpraising can set up a teenager for failure the next time they do something wrong, as they will feel that they have let you and themselves down, which increases their level of shame. A simple phrase like 'It is good to see you taking your glass to the kitchen' is more than enough.

Communication

Teenagers who undergo ACEs that lead to trauma are let down and betrayed by the very people who they should be able to trust the most – their birth parents. It should come as no surprise to anyone that they find it difficult to form relationships with other carers. Most teenagers who become part of the care system may have had several previous placements prior to joining your family. They often find it hard to engage in family activities and routines and struggle to participate in a basic, general conversation; to do so would be to relinquish some of their control, and they use control as a way of keeping themselves safe.

The best way to enable teenagers to let go of some of their need to feel in control is to make them feel safe. Doing this requires you to make a connection with the teenager. This will be covered in more detail when I discuss the topic of communicating with our teenagers in Section Three of this book. The process of making them feel safe can be initiated by the caregiver by approaching them with acceptance, showing empathy and being non-judgemental.

To support any child in feeling safe enough to engage in conversation with the parent involves the attitude of **PACE**: being **playful, accepting, curious and empathetic** (Golding & Hughes, 2012). PACE was developed by Dan Hughes, a clinical psychologist based in the United States who specialises in the treatment of children and young people who experienced abuse and neglect.

PACE was developed as a way of thinking, feeling, communicating and behaving to make the child feel safe. With PACE, children can start looking at themselves and letting others see them or get closer emotionally. In short, they can start to trust again. The principles of parenting with PACE are a great resource for parents or foster carers looking for guidance on interacting with children and young people in care, particularly those who experienced trauma. PACE, for me, is the foundation of therapeutic parenting, and it enables attunement between the teenager and the parent. Attunement is when two people share an emotional experience. The emotional connection between them happens when one person mirrors or matches the effect of the other. It is not the same as sharing an emotion. If a person is attuned to someone's despair, he is not in despair himself but is matching how the other is expressing their despair, for example, using a low tone of voice and employing a slow pace when speaking.

Playfulness

Playfulness is all about the tone of voice and establishing an atmosphere of gentleness and interest when you are communicating with teenagers. It requires you to develop the skill of speaking with a light tone and creating a calming effect through your voice (for instance, as though telling a story) instead of using an exasperated or lecturing tone. It is about having fun, expressing a sense of joy, and not making the teenagers feel that they are in any kind of trouble.

To apply playfulness, you must create a feeling of inner calm for yourself. You can do this by thinking of a happy time you had together, a time when you both were feeling relaxed and enjoying each other's company. It is important for you to get your mind into the right place before you speak to the teenager in your care. You want to create a situation/atmosphere in which neither of you feel judged or criticised. You want both of you to come out of this situation having sustained your relationship.

I outlined earlier in the book that trauma can result in teenagers finding it hard to regulate their feelings: anger becomes rage, fear becomes terror, and sadness becomes despair. Many teenagers who experienced abuse and neglect are not motivated enough to experience good times or share fun and enjoyment. They even feel incapable of giving or receiving a hug. If this is the case, the teenager may also find it hard to regulate feelings of excitement, joy and love. Feeling these emotions can sometimes lead to anxiety. Injecting a little playfulness will and does create space for a little amount of closeness, taking away the fear. Enabling teenagers to cope with positive feelings through a playful approach communicates to them that there is hope. It can also help teenagers develop or find their own sense of humour. They can then start to reflect on their own behaviour and what informs it. Laughter does stop individuals from being defensive or withdrawn and enables them to develop their own sense of self.

Having a playful stance is not about being funny all the time or making jokes when a teenager is sad. It is about helping children be more open to and experience what is positive in their life, one step at a time. A playful stance adds elements of fun and enjoyment in day-to-day life and can also diffuse a difficult or tense situation. The child is less likely to respond with anger and defensiveness when the parent adds a touch of playfulness to their disciplinary actions. While such a response would not be appropriate at the time of major misbehaviour, when applied to minor behaviours, playfulness can help keep it all in perspective. However, there may be times when a teenager starts shouting at you and injecting an element of playfulness stops them in their tracks and makes their anger turn into fits of laughter.

Playful moments reassure the teenager that although there were times of conflict/minor irritations and/or separation in the past, these were only temporary and will not harm the strength of your relationship.

Acceptance

I have mentioned in previous chapters the importance of accepting your teenagers for who they are. This does not mean that you should not have expectations or should establish boundaries regarding behaviour. When you accept their inner life, thoughts, feelings, hopes, judgements and memories, they are more likely to accept your boundaries and behaviours. To truly accept the teenagers in your care, it is important to consistently look beyond their behaviour. When they make derogatory comments about themselves, you are more than likely to find yourself wanting to respond, 'That is not right' or 'That is not true', or say the opposite to their claim. However, doing this is equal to not accepting how they see themselves or feel inside. The best approach is to accept what they say and/or feel and respond with curiosity and empathy. Reflecting what they experience will help establish a connection between you and them. Unconditional acceptance of the children in your care is the foundation of making them feel safe.

Accepting your teenagers' feelings and emotions does not mean that you are accepting their behaviour (which may indeed be quite harmful to you or others). Parents should be clear and consistent in addressing unsatisfactory behaviours while also accepting the reasons behind the behaviour. The intention here is to make your teenagers realise that while you are addressing their behaviours and putting natural consequences in place, this is solely because of their behaviours and not them as a person. Hopefully, after a period of time, they will become more confident that any differences or disagreements are based on behaviours, not on their relationship with you or your opinions of them.

Curiosity is the foundation of the acceptance of whatever underlies the behaviour. Making sense of how a child has learnt to behave in certain ways can help with acceptance.

Curiosity

I cannot stress enough the importance of being curious about your teenager's inner thoughts, feelings and intentions. Being curious about misbehaviour makes the natural consequence more effective. This needs to be done in an accepting tone, without judgement and, if appropriate, with a hint of playfulness. You should never ask the question 'why' for it is highly unlikely that your teenager will know why they acted in the way they did. Asking why just increases shame and can potentially create more anxiety. Your aim is not to try and establish facts or deliver a lecture; it is to try and offer understanding.

You can apply curiosity by saying such statements out loud: 'I wonder if . . .' or 'I'm guessing that . . .'. This is a good way of guessing what is going on as it lets the teenagers know that you are trying to understand. You may not always be right, but quite often, if you are not, they will open up a little, giving you a 'hook' to start exploring further in an empathetic manner. When making guesses out loud about what a teenager may be thinking or feeling, keep them connected to the present rather than the past. Never expect an answer; curiosity is a means of conveying that you are trying to understand what is happening for their sake. Very often, when you are being curious, it feels like you are having a conversation in the room, almost by yourself, with the teenager just listening. You will find that curiosity prevents frustration on both sides.

Your being curious instead of judgemental will aid you in conversation as it defuses any potential anger. By practicing curiosity, you can enable your teenagers to communicate their feelings, thereby reducing the need for a particular behaviour and the behaviour itself. Expression of feelings leads to a reduction in defensiveness and shame and an increase in guilt, which, in turn, decreases the frequency of that specific behaviour.

Couples can practise curiosity with each other when reflecting on any incidents that occur in a day. This will help you both stay empathised and attuned to the teenager in your care. Single carers can undertake this task with someone from their support bubble, applying the same principles.

Empathy

Empathy lets teenagers know that you feel compassion for them and that you want to try and understand how they are feeling. By being empathetic, you can show them that you actively care about their inner emotions, feelings and experiences, that they are of utmost importance to you, that you want to stand beside them in hard times and that when they are sad or in distress, you also feel sadness and distressed.

Sarah Naish (2018), in her amazing book, *The A to Z of Therapeutic Parenting*, gives some practical tips on how to actually demonstrate empathy through communication. It is usually done in the form of a commentary rather than direct questions. Even when teenagers are dysregulated, it is important to not challenge the behaviour; you must only address the underlying, deep-rooted issues.

What you do shows the young person that you are beside them. A series of useful phrases are listed below:

- It must be really tough to feel that way about x.
- I can see that you are finding this difficult.
- It must be so hard to feel that sad.
- It must be tough to feel that way about your mum.

Wondering out loud also enables you to say what you think is happening with your teenager in an empathetic way.

- I wonder if something happened today at school to make you feel so angry.
- I wonder if you are shouting because you want me to notice you.
- I wonder if you are angry because I asked you to take the bins out.

Undertaking this approach is so much more beneficial than asking direct questions and, more importantly, lets your teenager know that you are trying to understand what is happening to them instead of just focusing on their behaviour.

The most important aspect of empathy is that you are displaying strength, understanding and commitment with the confidence that the teenager's distress, anger and chaotic behaviour are not too much for you. Together, you will get through this, regardless of the current situation.

Summary of PACE

PACE focuses on the person as a whole and not just their behaviour. It helps teenagers feel more safe and secure while formulating a trusting relationship with their parenting figure. PACE supports them in reflecting on their feelings, emotions, thoughts and behaviours. This allows them to build the skills necessary to maintain a successful and satisfying future. They will start to realise that they are not worthless, lazy and selfish and that they are doing the best they can after being on an immensely difficult, traumatic journey.

PACE enables teenagers to slowly start trusting people, especially their parents, again, which is so hard for any teenager living with developmental trauma. PACE lets them see that their parents can look after them in a way that they cannot manage to on their own,

Using PACE most of the time will reduce the level of conflict, defensiveness and withdrawal that tends to be ever present in the lives of your troubled teenager. It enables you to see the strengths and positive features that lie underneath more negative and challenging behaviours. PACE is often seen as the bedrock of therapeutic parenting.

Conclusion

Therapeutic parenting focuses on trying to make the teenager in our care feel safe. This style of parenting places emphasis on high structure underpinned with nurture. Therapeutic parenting sees behaviour as a method of communication. It is about 'connected parenting', i.e. trying to connect with the teenager's feelings, emotions, fears, anxieties and traumatic memories. This is achieved by applying PACE. Therapeutic parents need to undertake purposeful actions and know why they are using a specific tool or strategy. Being a therapeutic parent is an intentional choice. Being intentional means having a plan in place, which also makes it easier to respond to your child and not react to behaviours. This style of parenting is effective, but it can take an exceptionally long time for the strategies to have an impact. Therapeutic parenting is very demanding for the parent and immensely time-consuming. Therefore, an essential component of therapeutic parenting is recognising when you need a break; breaks should be periodically added to the structure for they are beneficial for all parties involved in the parent–child relationship. This issue is explored in subsequent chapters.

Here are a few things in relation to therapeutic parenting that I have learnt from working and fostering young people over a long period of time. More information on how to apply these strategies is available on the Attachment & Trauma Network (ATN) website.

- Do not take the child or teenager's behaviours personally – it is not about you; it is about what happened to them.

- Do not forget to take care of yourself – exercise regularly and have your own identity by taking up another interest or hobby.

- Do not forget to extend to yourself the same patience and grace that you extend to your teenager.

- Remember that the teenager's behaviours are rooted in fear (and sometimes in shame); this fear is expressed as anger, aggression, violence and rejection.

- Remaining calm, regulated, and positive is the key to making any strategy successful.

- Remember, being a therapeutic parent most of the time is amazing. Well done, you!

- Build up a really solid support network for yourself.

- Build respite (breaks from your child) into your family's life. This is important for parents to ensure that they spend time together and with family and friends.

- Read, study and learn. Then practise, practise and practise again. You cannot become a therapeutic parent overnight.

I mentioned in the introduction of this book that even after numerous attempts at parenting therapeutically, I kept slipping back into old patterns, i.e., the way I had been parented and had previously parented children. Therefore, after a lot of reflection, I decided to train my mind so that it is able to react differently when faced with certain situations. What I was aiming to achieve was to therapeutically parent in the here and now, without having to give it much thought. I wanted to parent therapeutically unconsciously, rather than having to try consciously. The next section of this book focuses on training oneself to be a therapeutic parent.

TRAINING YOURSELF TO BE A THERAPEUTIC PARENT

Chapter 4:
MIND TRAINING

I have discovered, through trial and error, that to be a consistent therapeutic parent, one has to reprogramme their mind. This is due to the major differences between therapeutic parenting and the standard parenting approaches outlined in the previous chapters. Trust me, I have read all the books, attended training courses and watched numerous videos, but try as I might, I found myself slipping back into my old parenting style. I have since recognised that what is required is a method of training that will reprogramme one's mindset. The aim of mind training is to embed the therapeutic parenting approach into our subconscious mind through affirmations, creative visualisation and goal setting. This is then underpinned by emotional intelligence for both elements are interlinked; their working in tandem will enable us to consistently parent therapeutically.

Our brains have been built in such a way that they regulate our life. Our subconscious mind has something called a homeostatic impulse, which regulates crucial things such as body temperature, heartbeat and breathing. The homeostatic impulse, often referred to as the automatic nervous system, maintains the balance of chemicals within the billions of cells in our body. This keeps the body functioning and all the physical machine functions working in harmony. The brain regulates not only our physical self but also what happens to us mentally. Our mind relentlessly filters and brings to our attention information and stimuli that confirm our pre-existing beliefs, and it also presents us with repeated thoughts and impulses that imitate and mirror what we have previously experienced. This process is often referred to as 'confirmation bias' in the field of psychology (D, Siegel, 2012). Therefore, it is important for us to recognise that the role of our subconscious mind is that of a gatekeeper and that it does affect how we feel and react in certain situations. This does have major implications when changing your parenting style. If left unchecked, your subconscious mind will respond based on your past parental experiences and previous responses.

What you need to do is retrain your subconscious mind to act the way you want it to in certain situations. You need it to be able to filter challenging behaviours and routinely seek out therapeutic responses, informed by the learnt methods and strategies that underpin therapeutic parenting. This is not easy, and I am fairly confident that it will take an exceedingly long time to get your subconscious mind to react differently if you do not retrain your mind and solely rely on experiential learning.

Here are a few issues that need to be considered before you retrain your mind to be your collaborator and consistently respond in ways that are beneficial to your role as a therapeutic parent:

Embrace Change

The first step for being a therapeutic parent is to not just believe that it is possible but to be willing to see if it is. You have probably realised by now that you cannot change the way you parent overnight, but what you can do is be open to seeing if it will be possible after a period of time. This means that you are positioning yourself to embrace change.

Give Yourself Permission to Be a Therapeutic Parent

Instead of thinking to yourself, 'I wish I had not reacted the way I did to that behaviour' or 'I wish I had not responded in the manner I did', try a different dialogue, a dialogue that grants you permission to change. Change your inner dialogue to, 'Once I develop my skill of parenting therapeutically, things will be so much better for our family'. What you are actually doing is starting to break free from your subconscious's association with its pre-existing template of parenting. In a sense, you are giving yourself the permission to take a step in a different direction.

Disregard Other People's Views of Your Parenting Approach

I have spoken to many carers who parent therapeutically, and one of the challenges that always comes to the fore of the conversation is how they feel that others judge and/or perceive their therapeutic parenting approach. Therapeutic parenting is about addressing the feelings behind the behaviour rather than the behaviour itself. This can be really confusing to onlookers for you do not appear to be tackling the presented behaviours. I know carers who have experienced this while in supermarkets and restaurants, and they have seen other shoppers and/or diners being quite critical of their parenting approach. When I am out and about and see this myself, if the opportunity arises, I actually share with the parents how well I thought they tackled the situation. I often think to myself that unless someone has actually parented a traumatised child, they have no right to comment, but unfortunately, people do even otherwise.

Positive Reinforcement

Surround yourself with positive things and people. When you feel that you have really done well in managing situations therapeutically, give yourself a treat. Make sure to not let other individuals, in your immediate life and/or on social media, pull you down. When speaking about your successes, use the present tense rather than the future tense. Let me share an example of this from when I used to teach English as a second language. I would tell my students to not say, 'I want to be able to speak English'. I would instruct them to say, 'I speak English'. This was because the first statement will actually put barriers in their way, affect their confidence, and slow down their development. On the other hand, the second statement is a positive affirmation

Therapeutically Parenting Teenagers with Developmental Trauma

of what they can do, and this will build their confidence and enable them to develop quicker as English speakers. The same applies to therapeutic parenting. Surround yourself, if possible, with like-minded people, and join some groups or forums related to therapeutic parenting. An excellent Facebook group is The National Association of Therapeutic Parents (NATP).

Goals

Top-level athletes, successful businesspeople and achievers in all fields set goals. Setting goals for developing your therapeutic parenting skills gives you long-term vision and short-term motivation. It focuses your acquisition of knowledge and helps you organise your time and resources so that you can maximise the use of your time.

By setting sharp, clearly defined goals, you can measure and take pride in their achievements, and you will see progress in your own development as a therapeutic parent. Your self-confidence will increase as you recognise your own ability and competence in achieving the goals that you set. Goal setting is a powerful process that helps you think about how you will approach your aims and motivate yourself to turn your aims into reality (Morrison, 2014). After I took up the role of a therapeutic parent, I soon realised that I needed to map my progress to see how well I was progressing. I have previously used goal setting in other spheres of my life, and they helped me develop myself; so, it makes sense to undertake the same process while trying to become a better therapeutic parent. The process of setting goals is explained in more detail in Chapter 5.

Affirmations

Affirmations are specific positive suggestions you say to yourself to direct yourself towards your goals, build your self-confidence and maintain your motivation to reach your dreams. They are an intricate part of the mind-training process.

The more you repeat the affirmation, the greater the impact on your subconscious mind. We live in our conscious mind, so it will take some time before your affirmation actually embeds itself into your subconscious. It can take anywhere from 25 to 30 days of constant programming for it to become a part of your mental programme. The theory here is that if you keep telling yourself that you can do something, this will become a part of your subconscious before long (Fleming, 2020). The impact this can and will have on your confidence will be astounding. To maximise the benefits of affirmations, there are a set of guidelines that need to be followed. These will enable you to experience the true benefit of this form of positive thinking. These are explored in more details in Chapter 6.

Creative Visualisation

Combining affirmations and visualisation is a good way to speed up the process of influencing the subconscious mind as using both words and images is significantly more impactful.

Visualisation involves creating an image or a movie clip of sorts in our minds. In a way, you could call it daydreaming. Some people are better at this than others, but it seems that this skill can be worked upon and developed. How many times have you drifted off into a daydream? At times, the daydream is not clear and forms a clouded image, which is insignificant. However, there are times when you see everything in vivid detail; it is like looking at your aspiration unfolding in front of you and your desired outcomes getting fulfilled. You feel like you are outside yourself, looking at a sequence of events (Lorrison, 2014). This is not a hard process to develop but an immensely powerful one. I find it so beneficial when used alongside my affirmations. This will be explored in more detail in Chapter 7.

Eliminate Self-Doubt and Non-Therapeutic Reactions

Before exploring goals, affirmations and creative visualisation in more detail, I want to discuss the issue of self-doubt for I personally feel that this is an important factor of mind training.

Thoughts, feelings, attitudes, beliefs and imagination – all of these have an impact on how you parent. They are all inextricably linked to self-confidence but can also manifest as self-doubt. When faced with challenging situations, your subconscious mind, informed by your pre-existing beliefs and impulses, starts to filter and bring to your attention information and stimuli that imitate and reflect the times you dealt with challenging behaviours. You may recall that this is referred to as 'confirmation bias'. If left unchecked, this will start to put a subjective spin on how you want to react to the situations you face. What you need to realise is that your brain and mind can and often do operate in different time frames. Even while the brain operates in the present, the mind can linger in the past, forging possible past or future scenarios. It simply does not give your brain credit for possessing the ability to achieve different outcomes in the future. Self-doubt surfaces when you lack confidence in what you are trying to achieve; its fodder is past experience or mistakes, comparison with others and the fear of failure (Fleming, 2020).

Self-doubt leads to stress and anxiety, which triggers your fight-or-flight reflex; and while you often see this reflex in children and young people with developmental trauma, self-doubt makes you mirror the same types of reactions and behaviours. You respond to the challenging behaviour through an anxiety- and stress-informed parenting style rather than a trauma-informed one. You lose your focus on how you want to parent due to a lack of confidence in your abilities or self-doubt. In a sense, you mirror the behaviour shown by the teenager in your care though you wanted to concentrate on responding to the challenging behaviour by undertaking a therapeutic parenting approach.

So, what strategy or mind training can you adopt to deal with self-doubt and loss of concentration? On previous occasions, I followed the approach of telling myself to take a deep breath, try and settle the butterflies in my stomach, and then attempt to concentrate harder. I now realise that this was and still is a major mistake. Trying to concentrate actually means quite the opposite – that you are definitely not concentrating. The important factor here is that you must first accept and acknowledge the potential of your own parenting approach. You must have faith in your ability to be a therapeutic parent. This is often referred to as self-confidence. To enable this, you need to ensure that you are constantly focusing on the trauma-informed strategies that you know work and want to apply in this situation. At the same time, you must reduce and divert the irrelevant material generated by your subconscious mind in connection to pre-existing beliefs and impulses as they imitate and reflect the times you previously dealt with challenging behaviours.

I am sure that you have experienced that tight knot in your stomach as the fight-or-flight reflex starts to take hold due to the mind perceiving a confrontational situation (in this case, facing challenging behaviour). In such situations, you should try to explore what is actually happening. You need to 'ground' yourself and put the situation into context by asking the following question: 'What is actually happening here?' Think therapeutically: 'What is behind this behaviour? Do I really want to escalate this situation? How can I start to regulate the teenager's behaviour? More importantly, what are they trying to communicate?' Once you take a step back and get a reality check, you can start to take control of these powerful feelings.

Therapeutically Parenting Teenagers with Developmental Trauma

Part of taking control of these feelings is reflecting on what would be the ideal outcome of the situation. The last thing you want is for you and the teenager to end up shouting at the top of your voices and the situation concluding with the teenager slamming their bedroom door, telling you in no uncertain terms what to do. This is a no-win situation for both parties: No doubt, once the anger subsides, the teenager will still be experiencing anxiety, which will more than likely be coupled with shame. You will probably go and find refuge in a corner of the house, licking your wounds and feeling despondent. You will feel like a total failure as a parent for you did not intervene therapeutically; all you did was make the teenager feel worse. If a situation like this ever arises, you have to wait for the right time to present itself so you can repair the situation.

I am sure that you did not take up your parenting role to add to the anxiety and shame felt by children and young people with developmental trauma nor did you want to feel like a failure as a parent. On the contrary, I am sure that you want to be able to parent in such a way that the young person who joined your family can start to feel some sense of belonging and not live in constant fear. If you foster, adopt or operate under the guise of any of the other caring orders, you have made a challenging choice, and you have to be in it for the long haul, but the good times, which are so rewarding, definitely outweigh the challenging times.

Well, the good news is that there is a way to fight those feelings of self-doubt. Once you understand what is driving them, you can actually go ahead and do something about them: Bring in a different attitude. Accept that these feelings are natural and a part of the transition process when moving from one particular parenting style to another. Harnessing the feelings and, more importantly, understanding why they are happening can be to your advantage, and soon enough, they will enhance your commitment to being a therapeutic parent. Once you start perceiving self-doubt as an asset rather than a liability, you will see a major difference in your overall parenting.

Conclusion

Slowly but surely, self-doubt will cease to be a feature of your parenting style. When it does reappear, you can harness it by using the right mindset and attitude. This will enable you to make it a part of your parenting formula. Understanding that self-doubt can lead to stress and anxiety, which trigger our fight-or-flight reflex, is an especially important component of training our minds; it is only after this realisation that we can start embedding the techniques and strategies of therapeutic parenting into our subconscious minds. Tackling self-doubt is an important aspect of mind training. However, this is more effective when applied alongside other strategies such as goal setting, affirmations and creative visualisation.

Chapter 5:
GOAL SETTING

Picking up a copy of this book is a clear indicator of your desire to become a therapeutic parent. Dreams and desires are important in life, and quite often, they are linked to goals. However, I do think that there is a difference between desires and goals. We can dream all day about sitting under a parasol on a beautiful beach, but that is not going to make it happen. Wishful thinking is not goal setting. The main difference here is that goal setters make firm decisions and write things down to achieve the set goals, whereas wishful thinkers never reach that stage. What prompts goal setters to write things down is ambition.

Writing down your goal sends a clear message to your brain, and when the opportunity to achieve your goal arises and your desire is high, you will find that you can concentrate better and are more likely to apply the appropriate therapeutic strategy in any given situation. Writing goals down gives them a concrete form, and the note serves as a reminder and a reference point for you when progressing in your journey as a therapeutic parent. You become assured of your own abilities, and this will fuel your concentration. You will not only feel confident about acting therapeutically but also start seeing better outcomes when faced with challenging situations.

The Process of Goal Setting

Most individuals start by writing down their long-term goals. In this case, it could be 'I want to be the best therapeutic parent I can be'. Remember that the long-term goal marks the culmination of your journey. I think that we never stop learning and reach the end, but it is important to identify milestones along the way. Here, your long-term goal would act as your end point for this specific milestone. However, to identify how far you have progressed, you will also need a starting point. Every journey must have a beginning and an end. What is important is how you map out your journey.

Review

Before setting any goals, it is important to review and evaluate your current performance because the goals that you set will be performance related. To evaluate my own performance as a therapeutic parent, I undertook such an honest review. Within the review, you should explore your feelings and emotions, especially since setting goals constitutes an intricate part of mind training. Undertaking a review will enable you to identify your strengths and acknowledge the parts of your parenting approach that you need to develop to improve your performance. The review will show you things you had not previously considered or were aware of but didn't pay attention to. It will become the starting point in your journey to improvement as a therapeutic parent. I have supplied a series of questions that will be helpful in organising your review (Table 1). Please feel free to add more questions that you find suitable. The more detailed your review is, the more insightful it will be.

The mere act of writing down the answers to these questions will make your thinking focused. At the same time, you will have affirmed how badly you want to improve as a therapeutic parent. These answers will offer you an insight into the areas of your parenting that you need to improve on while making you aware of your mindset under any given situation. One of the biggest challenges you can face when embarking on a long journey is maintaining your self-motivation. How can you retain the same enthusiasm you had at the outset? The best way to do this is to set long, intermediate and short-term goals.

Table 1. Potential questions for a performance review

HISTORY	ANSWERS	PERFORMANCE	ANSWERS
1. How long have you been therapeutically parenting?		10. Would you say you are a below average, average or above average therapeutic parent?	
2. What got you interested in Therapeutic Parenting?		11. Do you think you are developing as a therapeutic parent?	
3. What did you achieve in your fist six months of Therapeutic Parenting?		12. How do rate a) your nurturing skills b) your curiosity skills?	
TEMPERAMENT	**ANSWERS**	13. What are your weaknesses at therapeutic parenting?	**ANSWERS**
4. Are you a positive person?		14. What is your proudest moment/intervention while parenting therapeutically?	
5. How well do you cope with extremely challenging behaviour?		15. How did you feel before, during and after your proudest moment/intervention while parenting therapeutically?	
6. Are you a confident person?		16. How consistent are you as a therapeutic parent?	
7. How often do you lose your temper?		**GENERAL**	
8. How do you prepare for therapeutic parenting mentally?		17. How good are you at taking care of yourself on a scale of 1 to 10, with 10 being highest?	
9. Do you experience self-doubt about your therapeutic parenting skills?		18. How high is your commitment level to improve on a scale of 1 to 10, with 10 being highest?	

Therapeutically Parenting Teenagers with Developmental Trauma

SMART Goals

Having understood the benefits of writing down goals, it is important to consider the rules of goal setting. I am sure that many of you have already been introduced to the concept of setting SMART goals, which can add structure to your goals and make them trackable. Instead of a series of vague resolutions, you will have a set of clear milestones and an estimation of the goal's attainability. Every goal can be made into a SMART goal.

SMART is an acronym for specific, measurable, achievable, realistic and time-bound. A SMART goal incorporates all of these aspects to help focus your efforts and increase the chances of success. Below is a breakdown of the process I use when setting SMART goals. I start by asking myself the following questions (I have included an example of a goal for each set of questions):

Specific

Goals that are specific have a significantly greater chance of being accomplished. To make a goal specific, ask yourself the following five 'W' questions:

Who: Who is involved in this goal?

What: What do I want to accomplish?

Where: Where is this goal to be achieved?

When: When do I want to achieve this goal?

Why: Why do I want to achieve this goal?

Example: I will sit down in a quiet space with my foster daughter four times a week to give her my undivided attention and improve the quality of our relationship.

Measurable

A SMART goal must include criteria to measure progress. If there are no criteria, you will not be able to determine your progress or whether you are on track to reach your goal. To make a goal measurable, ask yourself this:

How many/much?

How do I know if I have reached my goal?

What is my indicator of progress?

Example: I will read one book per month on therapeutic parenting and monitor how this impacts my parenting through my weekly logs.

Achievable

A SMART goal must be achievable and attainable. This will help you figure out ways in which you can realise that goal and work towards it. The achievability of the goal should be expanded to such a degree that it challenges you and defined well enough for you to achieve it. Now ask yourself this:

Do I possess the resources and capabilities to achieve the goal? If not, what am I missing?

Have others done it successfully before?

Example: To set clear and concise boundaries in negotiation with our foster daughter, monitor their effectiveness and review monthly

Realistic

A SMART goal must be realistic, meaning that we must be able to realistically achieve it given the available resources and time. A SMART goal is likely to be realistic if you believe that it can be accomplished. Now ask yourself:

Is the goal realistic and within reach?

Is the goal reachable given the time and resources?

Am I able to commit to achieving the goal?

Example: I will keep a daily log of how I feel I therapeutically parented each day. The log will be used in my supervision sessions with my supervising social worker.

Time-bound

A SMART goal must be time-bound in that it must have a start and finish date. If the goal is not constrained by time, there will be no sense of urgency and motivation to achieve the goal. Ask yourself:

Does my goal have a deadline?

By when do I want to achieve my goal?

Example: By the end of September 2021, I will have completed Level 1 of my therapeutic parenting course.

In any goal-setting exercise, your starting point is to form your long-term goal as that defines the end point of your journey. This is supplemented by your intermediate and short-term goals. Using the information from your review, i.e., focusing on your answers to the set questions, will enable you to complete the goal-setting task. You should never set too many goals for yourself – therapeutic parenting is a journey, not a sprint. You will need one long-term goal that is underpinned by a number of intermediate goals. An example of a long-term goal could be to be the best therapeutic parent you can be. Once you have set your goal, write it down on a basic chart (Table 2), and display it where you will see it every day. This will be extremely useful for having your goals in view does enable you to reflect on how therapeutic your interactions have been with the teenager in your care.

Long-term Goal

Once you have set your long-term goal, you are on your way to achieving it. This should not be an over-complicated process. Remember, you write goals to stay motivated and focused and to monitor your progression as a therapeutic parent. Writing them down and seeing them every day does grant you a sense of direction and will help move the goals from your conscious into your subconscious. Your long-term goal is the final step in your journey, your ultimate destination. Achieving it will require you to take a series of steps, which are a succession of intermediate and short-term goals to be conquered.

Intermediate Goals

Intermediate goals serve as the milestones in your journey. In a sense, your intermediate goals are the stepping stones on your path to achieving your long-term goal. Take care not to confuse these with day-to-day short-term goals. Aim to set around six intermediate goals every year.

You should write your intermediate goals on your chart in descending order. Your last and final intermediate goal should go directly under the long-term goal. The other intermediate goals should be placed in reverse order. Thus, your first intermediate goal will be at the bottom of the chart. I recommend having columns to record the dates and how you actually fared when tackling each of the intermediate goals. Your chart becomes your master plan (Table 2). Therefore, you need to see it daily. It is also your monitoring tool for checking and mapping out your progress. Constantly reviewing your chart will enable you to stay motivated. There will be times when external factors, i.e. factors beyond your control, affect your achievements. Do not be too hard on yourself – all you need to do is adjust your plan. This is your own, personal plan that will be different from others'.

Short-term Goals

The best way to start working on your short-term goals is to look at your first intermediate goal in your chart and ask yourself this question: 'Why have I not achieved it yet?' I am sure that once you ask yourself this question, what you need to do next will become apparent. You will soon realise that to achieve your first intermediate goal, you will have to focus on a series of daily activities as a part of your routine. What you have actually produced is a set of short-term goals that need your immediate attention, and this will ensure that each day is focused and has clear outcomes. Below are examples of two short-term goals. These have been set to improve a carer's application of natural consequences. These are part of what they need to improve to partially achieve their intermediate goal of 'only setting natural consequences to help develop cause and effect' with their foster daughter. Here is how they set short-term goals that are linked to the specific intermediate goal.

'To only determine natural consequences that help develop cause and effect with our foster daughter' (intermediate goal), I need to do the following:

- Use the three Rs method when setting natural consequences to ensure that each consequence is related to the behaviour and is respectful and reasonable.

- After setting each natural consequence, I will make sure that, when appropriate, I have a brief discussion with our foster daughter to link cause and effect.

I suggest not adding the short-term goals to your chart; they should be recorded separately, preferably under the heading of the intermediate goal you are working towards. This should be displayed alongside your chart.

Below is an example of a chart (Table 2) of a foster carer who set herself the long-term goal of being a competent foster carer. She is fairly new to fostering, so her chart is not that detailed. What is important is that she has set herself a long-term goal and a series of intermediate goals that will help her progress on her fostering journey as a therapeutic parent. Each intermediate goal has a series of short-term goals.

Table 2. Example of a goal-setting chart

GOAL CHART			
GOAL	**SUCCESS CRITERIA**	**EVIDENCE/ACHIEVED**	**DATE/ACHIEVED**
Long-term goal			
To become a competent therapeutic foster carer.	To think and act therapeutically for the majority of the time- positive impacts on the children in my care.		
Intermediate goals	**SUCCESS CRITERIA**	**EVIDENCE/ACHIEVED**	**DATE/ACHIEVED**
To be confident in applying the principle of PACE by the end of October 2020.	Confidently applying Playfulness, Acceptance, Curiosity and Empathy.		
To be an empathic listener by mid-June 2020.	Being able to listen without giving opinions.		
To be able to recognise the symptoms of Compassion Fatigue by April 2020.	Attend training course-read books. Recognise signs and signals of compassion fatigue. Build in regular self-care activities.		
Educate all members of my support bubble about the basics of trauma and how it impacts children by the end of March 2020.	Discussion held with all members of my support bubble – literature distributed.		
To set clear negotiated boundaries by the beginning of March 2020.	Effective boundaries in place and working effectively.		
Attend course on Therapeutic Parenting by end of February 2020.	Course completed.	Achieved a good understanding from the course. Applying the basic principles of TP.	End of Feb 2020.

Conclusion

Goal setting is an especially important component of mind training. Setting goals helps trigger new behaviours, guide your focus and sustain progression. Goals not only align your focus but also help promote self-mastery, in this case, in therapeutic parenting. Realistically, you cannot manage what you cannot measure, and you cannot improve upon something that you do not effectively manage. Setting goals will enable you to achieve this and more.

Chapter 6:
AFFIRMATIONS

As previously discussed, the subconscious mind is the part of one's mind that operates below the normal level of waking consciousness. Right now, you are using your conscious mind to read these words and absorb their meaning; beneath that mental focus, your subconscious mind is busily working to absorb or reject information based on your existing perception of the world. This existing perception began forming when you were a child.

How can affirmations and creative visualisation change this? When we repeat positive affirmations to ourselves, we train our brains to believe what we are saying. If you tell yourself 'I am confident' over and over again, you will soon start to feel more confident. The same principle applies to you telling yourself over and over again that you are scared of snakes. This manifests itself in your reality, and soon, you will feel afraid whenever you see a snake. You have told your brain that you are afraid of something, so your brain causes your body to react with fear.

How Do Affirmations Work?

We previously defined an affirmation as a specific positive suggestion you say to yourself to direct yourself towards your goals, build your self-confidence and maintain your motivation to reach your dreams. Your brain's ability to change and adapt to different circumstances throughout your life offers a clue to help us understand not only what makes affirmations work but also how we can make them more effective. Sometimes, your brain gets reality and imagination mixed up, which can be surprisingly useful. Regular repetition of affirmative statements about yourself can encourage your brain to take these positive affirmations as fact. When you honestly believe that you can do something, your actions often follow. For example, you might replace a negative or anxious statement with something positive:

'I am so terrible at interviews. I am probably not even as qualified as the other candidates. Really, there is no point in me turning up for the interview', can be replaced with, 'I have all the necessary skills and experience, and I am the perfect candidate for this job'.

Obviously, this change will not happen immediately for you will have to repeat the affirmation over a period of time to embed the thought into your subconscious. It can take anywhere from 25 to 30 days of constant repetition for it to become a part of your mental programme (Lively, 2014). The theory here is that if you keep telling yourself that you can do something, it becomes a part of your subconscious before long. Eventually, using affirmations may help you feel more relaxed before your interview, and knowing that you are fully prepared can also help you avoid self-sabotaging thoughts or behaviours that can potentially interfere with your success.

Affirmations generally work as a tool for shifting your mindset and achieving your goals, but they are not a magic injection for instant success. You have a role to play in ensuring that change does take place. Most importantly, once you change your mindset, you need to act. Repeating an affirmation can help boost your motivation and confidence, but you still have to take some action yourself. Try thinking of affirmations as a step towards change, not the change itself. For example, using affirmations to help yourself react differently when facing challenging behaviour will, hopefully, change your mindset. Instead of making you react in a way that could lead to a teenager feeling shame, your subconscious mind will help reinforce the need to act therapeutically. Once you have changed your mindset, the next step is to act therapeutically and see your actions through to achieve a better outcome.

To maximise the benefits of affirmations, a set of guidelines need to be followed. The following guidelines will enable you to experience the true benefit of this form of positive thinking (Lim, 2020).

Affirmations Must Be Positive

The language used in any affirmation must be positive. So, refrain from using words such as 'hope', 'try', 'wish' or other words suggesting indecisiveness. You must ensure that you keep it positive by using words such as 'when', 'I can', 'I will' and others that will create positive images of success in your mind. It is not the words but the images that have the power to eventually influence change.

Affirmations Must Be Stated in the Present Tense

You must choose the correct tense when saying your affirmation. It is essential to do this for all affirmations. So, rather than saying 'I will be confident', say 'I am confident', which is a more powerful affirmation that also includes the assumption that it will come true, that it is just a question of when.

Declare Affirmations Out Loud With Conviction

Affirmations are more effective when they are spoken out loud as they summon your willpower. This infuses your words with energy, belief and passion. A useful exercise is to stand tall in front of a mirror with your shoulders pulled back, look yourself directly in the eyes and say your affirmation with conviction (Lim, 2020).

I have personally used affirmations not only to help with the transition of my parenting styles but also in other areas of my life. Later in the book, when exploring self-care, I mention how I like to go crown green bowling and use the technique of repeating affirmations to improve my confidence, which always took a nosedive right before a competitive game. My low confidence affected my performance, and I would find myself considerably behind before I actually started playing to the best of my ability. The inevitable happened – I regularly lost by a significant margin. Having suffered the same pattern of losses for quite some time, I started practicing a series of affirmations, following the recommended guidelines. This did have a major impact on my performance, and I started to win on a regular basis, seeing further improvements with time. I attributed this to my confidence level being high at the beginning of each game, enabling me to start scoring from the outset. You could argue that this would have happened anyway with more games as greater experience results in increased confidence. But I do not think that this was the case; I am certain that using affirmations made a major difference in my confidence. As for how this came about, whether it was due to believing in the positive-thinking approach or the increased experience, I simply do not care. What is important is that I achieved my desired outcome.

Even though you might not feel the affirmation on some days, do not let this deter you for you must consistently undertake the daily process. I came across one piece of good advice while reading about affirmations: 'Fake it until you make it'. Believe me, consistency does count. The more you repeat the affirmation, the greater the impact on your subconscious mind. We live in our conscious mind, so it will take some time before your affirmation actually embeds itself into your subconscious. As previously mentioned, it can take anywhere from 25 to 30 days of constant programming for it to become a part of your mental programme. The theory here is that if you keep telling yourself that you can do something, before long, it will become a part of your subconscious. The impact this will have on your confidence will be astounding.

Conclusion

Combining affirmations with visualisation is a good way to speed up the process of influencing the subconscious mind as the combination of words and images is significantly more powerful than words or images alone. I have no doubt that using affirmations coupled with creative visualisation will really help you transition from a standard parenting style to a therapeutic one. You will be amazed at how you grow in confidence and how you find yourself responding therapeutically without giving it a second thought.

Using your goal chart as a template for identifying which affirmations you will practise next will help you keep progressing and improving in your performance. Reflecting on what you need to do to achieve your intermediate goal points you in the right direction for identifying your next short-term goal. You will find it beneficial to formulate your affirmations around the identified short-term goal.

I have previously stated that creative visualisation goes hand in hand with affirmations as these two forms of positive thinking share a close link and interface closely with goal setting in mind training. Therefore, the next chapter explores creative visualisation in depth.

Chapter 7:

CREATIVE VISUALISATION

Visualisation has become the norm for those wishing to excel in almost any area of sport and even in certain areas of medicine. Many athletes have shared how they visualise a game before it takes place, imagining how well they are going to perform. One thing that encourages athletes is feeling victorious. The positive emotions resulting from the creative visualisation of victory may give them that extra energy they need to take charge of their bodies and minds.

The practice of clinical guided imagery, or visualisation, is used in various ways. For several years now, it has been employed to help individuals heal their physical bodies and emotional states. Numerous studies have shown how beneficial this practice can be. It is not meant to take the place of traditional medical interventions, but it can certainly add to them. It is also a great tool for relaxation, which can be particularly challenging for anyone going through physical or emotional distress (Davenport, 2018).

In the previous chapter, I discussed the benefits of linking affirmations and creative visualisation based on the goals you have set yourself to improve your skill base as a therapeutic parent. I am a great believer of the idea that when you set yourself a goal, you need to identify what achieving it feels and looks like. Without this, how will you really know that you have achieved it? I think that this is where visualisation is extremely useful; it grants you experience. In a way, once you have seen your goal, you are geared towards attaining it. You also know that it is within your reach, and you will soon be well on your way to achieving it.

To put affirmation and visualisation into practice, I recommend setting yourself two sessions per day, each no longer than five minutes. Facing the mirror, look directly into your eyes and say your affirmation out loud three times. Then sit down and relax using the breathing technique outlined below. Then, go through your movie clip that visualises your affirmation. Embellish it, and make it as vivid as possible.

Undertaking the process of creative visualisation is not difficult. In its simplest form, it involves the following: To begin the process, sit in a comfortable position in a quiet place, and close your eyes. You do not have to be in a meditative state at this point. Breathe out until your lungs feel empty. Then, inhale through your nose, first filling your stomach and then the bottom section of your lungs, followed by the middle and, finally, the top of your lungs. Hold that for a count of five. Now, slowly exhale through your mouth. Feel your body relaxing, releasing all tension as you exhale. Let all your worries fall away. Let go of any distress in your body. Repeat three cycles of this deep breathing exercise.

Once you're in a relaxed state, visualise your goal in your mind's eye – think about what you want to develop as a therapeutic parent in relation to a specific goal from your goal chart. Then, begin with one small element of that desire and embellish it. What else would you add to your vision? What would render it more tangible to you? Be as specific as possible.

For example, visualise your teenager coming in one hour late, an hour after their curfew time. You had prepared them a meal, but it has gone cold. You are a little irritated for it did take quite a lot of preparation, and now that they are late, it will need to be reheated, and this will make you miss a considerable part of the favourite TV programme you had been looking forward to watching for most of the day. The door opens, and you feel the tension build up inside you. They walk through the door. They tell you in no uncertain terms that they do not care that they are late and that the curfew time makes them feel like a child rather than a grown-up. Focus on how you feel; acknowledge your anger, but do not let it take over. Attune yourself again. Think about what is behind this behaviour. What is it trying to communicate? Your first feeling is probably the urge to reprimand them for being late and then to complain that you have wasted your time preparing them a nice meal. Stop! The last thing you want to do is inflict more shame. Rather than ask why they are late, 'wonder' out loud about what has made them late. Show some empathy about how curfews can be problematic, especially when they are earlier than some of their friends'. Say out loud, as if speaking to yourself, the dilemma you face because you want them to have a fun time with their friends but also want to keep them safe. Focus on their reaction. See how their barriers come down, the change in their body stance. The most important thing is that they are home and safe and that you have avoided confrontation. Now is the time to inject some playfulness. Later, you might explore a natural consequence so that cause and effect are linked, if you feel that this is necessary.

Try to retain these images – play them over and over again in your mind. This is in preparation for your actual encounter with this or similar situations in real life. Prior to undertaking the visualisation, you need to state your affirmation out loud three times.

So, what are the actual benefits of using affirmation and visualisation in the process of therapeutic parenting? How can it practically supplement one's parenting style?

In an earlier chapter, I explored the different techniques we can use to block out the voice of self-doubt and concentrate on the here and now. Visualising is such a technique. When you focus on a good book, you may not hear the clock ticking until someone brings it to your attention. Similarly, you can use visualisation as a means to regain your focus and avoid being distracted from thinking and acting therapeutically. I am sure that you must have faced exceedingly challenging situations as a parent. The fight-or-flight reflex kicks in, and we all know what comes next. This is where visualisation can be of great benefit. You have played this movie clip over and over again in your mind – maybe not the exact situation but one remarkably similar, with the same amount of pressure attached. In your clip, you were fully relaxed and confident; you took your time and responded therapeutically, and you can now do the same in reality.

With visualisation, what you are aiming to achieve is to therapeutically parent, in the here and now, without having to give it much thought. You need to therapeutically parent unconsciously rather than having to try consciously. Trust me, your brain can be taught how to achieve this through affirmations and creative visualisation. In a sense, our brains can operate on autopilot, which is result of something often referred to as the default mode network (DMN) (Buckner, 2015).

The human brain is a truly fascinating organ: It handles so many of our daily actions without us having to even think about them. How often have you taken the same daily commute only to realise that you cannot remember or recall any part of it? Your brain went into autopilot while you were busy considering or doing something else. Scientists discovered that when the mind wanders, it switches to 'autopilot' mode, enabling you to perform tasks quickly, accurately and without conscious effort. Autopilot mode seems to be run by a set of brain structures called the DMN. When the brain is in this mode, it is actually assessing past events and planning for the future. It enters a state of consciousness. Evidence has shown that your responses become faster and more accurate due to DMN (Buckner, 2015). Through creative visualisation, you can reprogramme your subconscious mind to make it act in a therapeutic way rather than on what you have previously experienced. All you need to do is supply your brain with the appropriate therapeutic parenting strategies over a sustained period of time by setting goals, repeating affirmations and using creative visualisation methodologies. Training your mind and supplying it with endless amounts of therapeutic parenting information on an ongoing basis will improve its ability to support you in responding therapeutically.

Conclusion

Goal setting, affirmations and visualisation are all important methods of retraining your subconscious mind. Creative visualisation is a really powerful tool when combined with affirmations. The human brain should never be underestimated; in a sense, it is your own personal computer. All you have to do is programme it to respond to behaviours from a trauma-informed perspective, which will then enhance your therapeutic parenting skill base. Further, if you really want to embed a therapeutic parenting approach into your subconscious, you do need to prioritise working on understanding emotions. This will involve exploring and developing your emotional intelligence, which is discussed in the following chapter.

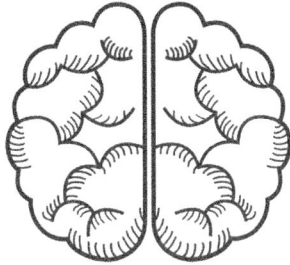

Self-Awareness

Motivation

Empathy

Social Skills

Self-Regulation

Emotional Intelligence

Chapter 8:

EMOTIONAL INTELLIGENCE

I am sure that we all know someone who seems to be able to stay calm under even in most immense pressure situations. Such people are able to handle the most awkward social situations with charm and always make others feel at ease. They are the calmest parents, and they never seem to be fazed by the behaviours their child exhibits. It is highly likely that these individuals possess high emotional intelligence.

Emotional intelligence involves the ability to understand and manage emotions. While having the ability to express and control emotions is essential, so is possessing the ability to understand, interpret and respond to the emotions of others. Experts agree that this type of intelligence plays an important role in success, and some have suggested that emotional intelligence might even be more important than IQ. Possessing emotional intelligence skills has been linked to good outcomes in everything, from decision-making to academics.

So, what does it take to be emotionally intelligent? Psychologist and author Daniel Goleman (1998) suggested that there are five components of emotional intelligence:

- Self-awareness
- Self-regulation
- Internal motivation

- Empathy
- Social skills

Fortunately, he outlined that everyone has the potential to work on and increase each individual skill to become more emotionally intelligent (Goleman, 2020).

According to the book *Discovering Psychology* by Don and Sandra Hockenbury (2007), an emotion is a complex psychological state that involves three distinct components: a subjective experience, a physiological response and a behavioural or expressive response.

For the purpose of this book and to link emotional intelligence with mind training, it will be beneficial to look at each of the five components identified by Goleman separately. Doing this will enable you to identify strategies that can help you improve in these skills while placing a specific focus on therapeutic parenting.

Self-Awareness

Self-awareness is having the ability to be aware of different aspects of oneself, i.e. one's behaviours, feelings, emotions and characteristics. Having the ability to recognise and understand your emotions is an essential part of emotional intelligence. It is essential to not only recognise your own emotions but also understand the effects of your emotions, actions and moods on others. This also entails being able to name emotions clearly and concisely.

To become self-aware, you must be able to acknowledge and monitor your emotions as well as your different reactions in relation to them. This requires you to differentiate and separately analyse each emotion. Being self-aware means that you can identify the relationship between what you feel and how it makes you behave, that you can recognise your own strengths while also accepting your limitations, that you are always open to new information and experiences and that you have a willingness to learn from others. Goleman (2020) suggested that people who possess self-awareness have a good sense of humour, are confident in themselves and their abilities and are aware of how other people perceive them. You can see how self-awareness is key in undertaking the role of a therapeutic parent because recognising our emotions and the impact they can have on others will determine what feelings we evoke in the child and our ability to keep them regulated.

Strategies for Improving Self-awareness

You can employ a number of strategies to improve your self-awareness and gain a better insight into how you react in different situations. Keeping a journal/diary is a good start. I would suggest doing this consistently and ensuring that you do not only record events but also explore your thoughts and feelings towards particular experiences. Keeping a journal will also help clarify your thoughts and feelings, giving you valuable self-knowledge.

Therapeutically Parenting Teenagers with Developmental Trauma

I have previously mentioned self-doubt as something that you need to be aware of when embarking on mind training. You may recall that I shared with you strategies for addressing this problem because, as we acknowledged, it can have a negative impact on you when facing challenging behaviours. However, an important part of self-awareness is making yourself mindful of self-talk. You might not even know that you are doing it. Self-talk is your inner voice that makes sense of the world around you. I personally feel that it is one of the most important aspects of self-awareness – how you make sense of your own world and the world around you will affect the way you communicate with your inner self. If your self-talk is generally negative, you will find yourself perceiving events in your life as more stressful than they need to be, which will impact your anxiety levels. You will also attribute negative motives to individuals who mean well; you may think of yourself as less equipped to handle the challenges you face, and you may see more negatives than positives in what you are facing in life. Being aware of your self-talk enables you to actually do something about it. It is possible to change negative self-talk into positive self-talk, which then becomes a benefit remarkably similar to positive affirmations.

Another way of developing self-awareness is mindfulness. It is the practice of becoming more or fully aware of the present moment non-judgmentally. It is about thinking about the here and now. It is about exploring what is fuelling your feelings and emotions rather than dwelling in the past or projecting on to the future. It generally involves a heightened awareness of your breathing, feeling the sensations of your body, etc. Making these connections will enable you to reflect on what emotions are behind your behaviours, which will, in turn, raise your awareness (Scott, 2020).

Mindset is exceptionally important in the context of emotional intelligence. It refers to whether you believe that qualities such as intelligence and talent are fixed or changeable. Doctor Carol Dweck (2016) identified two different mindsets with regard to individuals. People with a fixed mindset believe that these qualities are inborn, fixed and unchangeable. Those with a growth mindset, on the other hand, believe that these abilities can be developed and strengthened through commitment and hard work. The point here is to reflect on what type of mindset you possess as this will inform your self-awareness. Without a doubt, transitioning to a whole new parenting approach will require a growth mindset.

Emotional self-awareness is not something that you can achieve once and be done with. Rather, every moment is an opportunity to be self-aware. You need to build it into your conscious state as a therapeutic parent. The good news is that the more you do it, the more natural it will feel. The expected outcome is to be more 'open' to learning new skills and, while doing so, to pay attention to your thoughts and feelings. The key here is to reflect on your experiences. You will also find that you gain more benefits from your goal chart if you are more self-aware, which will ultimately make you a more emotionally intelligent therapeutic parent.

Self-Regulation

In addition to being aware of your own emotions and the impact you have on others, emotional intelligence requires you to regulate and manage your emotions. This does not mean locking down your emotions or trying to block them out; on the contrary, self-regulation is about expressing your emotions appropriately.

Goleman (1998) acknowledged that those who are skilled in self-regulation are flexible and can adapt to change quickly. He also identified that they are good at managing conflicts and diffusing awkward situations. He suggested that those with strong self-regulation skills are high in conscientiousness and that such individuals are organised, determined and able to postpone immediate gratification for the sake of long-term success. They are thoughtful about how they influence others and, so, are keen to take responsibility for their own actions. When someone is conscientious, they are able to exercise self-discipline and self-control to pursue and ultimately achieve their goals. All this shows how beneficial emotional regulation is for those therapeutically parenting a teenager with developmental trauma.

We all feel emotions, both negative and positive, on a daily basis. While developing as children, the majority of us learn to manage, cope and express our emotions in a healthy way. I have previously identified that children and/or young people who undergo ACEs such as abuse or trauma do find it extremely difficult to regulate their emotions. Knowing how to regulate your emotions is important for everyone, but what is emotional regulation, and what skills are required to do this successfully?

Though it is considered an important area of study and many have researched it in the field of psychology, there is still no agreed-upon definition of the term 'emotional regulation'. Many researchers have tried to define it, and a few suggestions have been put forward. For example, emotional regulation has been defined as the ability to enhance or suppress your emotions as and when needed. Other researchers use a much broader definition, viewing it as a means of keeping your emotional system healthy and functioning. Still others define it as something that occurs when an objective is activated. An objective is something that is specific to different individuals, something that they picture inside their minds – in a sense, they picture the way they would like to see something turn out. The researchers believe that objectives can be activated due to one's environment, which includes images, objects, words and sounds, and in a conscious or subconscious state (Kendra, 2021).

Here are some examples of activated objectives that can trigger the regulation of your emotions:

Influencing a Change in Someone Else

As a parent, your objective may be to help your teenager learn how to regulate their emotions. Accordingly, when they feel angry, upset or amused, you regulate your own emotions to respond accordingly instead of reflexively getting angry and yelling or falling into fits of laughter. This is referred to as extrinsic emotional regulation. However, sometimes the objectives can overlap. For example, speaking calmly and soothingly to an angry teenager (extrinsic) can actually decrease your own anger (intrinsic). You may recall that I raised this point when I discussed using playfulness to regulate both the teenager and yourself. I visit these concepts of extrinsic and intrinsic in more detail when I discuss motivation later on.

Influencing a Change in Yourself

If your objective is to be more positive, you may attain it by shifting your focus from a negative emotion to a positive one. Controlling your own emotions is known as intrinsic emotional regulation. This can be driven by certain cultural factors, i.e., what are viewed as good or bad feelings in your culture. Sometimes, you are expected to show certain emotions depending on a specific situation. Weddings and funerals are good examples of this.

Meeting Long-term Objectives

You may also regulate your emotions to achieve a long-term objective. For instance, imagine that the teenager in your care has once again left all their dirty washing strewn around their bedroom rather than in the wash basket. Having told them about this on numerous occasions, you feel angry and let down inside. However, you make the conscious decision to say nothing. You choose to regulate your emotions; you are aware that they are struggling

Therapeutically Parenting Teenagers with Developmental Trauma

emotionally because they have to meet their birth family later on that afternoon, which is always difficult for them. Therefore, considering the situation, your long-term objective is to keep them regulated prior to the meeting.

Changing the Intensity, Duration or Type of Emotion

Sometimes, we try to decrease or increase the intensity of our emotions. An example of this could be feeling anxious and worried because the teenager in your care has not returned home and that you might have to report them as missing to the police. The best thing to do then is to try and busy yourself to keep your mind occupied. What you are trying to do is block out the emotion of worrying by doing something else, which will hopefully help take your mind of the issue of them missing.

Sometimes, teenagers can give rise to emotions that you find extremely challenging. The behaviour that they exhibit has an impact on your emotions, and this can last for a long period of time in such cases, you have to reduce the intensity of the emotion through emotional acceptance. This is covered later on in this chapter. You can also show a different emotion than the one you are experiencing, for example, falling down in front of everyone can be very embarrassing; instead of showing your embarrassment in this case, you can laugh it off and make a big joke about it.

Unconscious Regulation

As the name suggests, this kind of emotional regulation happens without you even knowing or realising it; it takes place in your subconscious mind. It is like changing a TV channel, which happens at the click of a button. This is the state you would like to attain as therapeutic parents and use when faced with challenging behaviour. Achieving this will mean reprogramming your subconscious mind through mind training and gaining emotional intelligence. Understanding the impact of trauma, recognising that behaviour is a form of communication, setting goals, repeating affirmations, visualising creatively, dealing with self-doubt and thinking therapeutically are all part of this process.

A number of other techniques can be used to regulate emotions. These are briefly explored below to enhance your emotional regulation skills.

Techniques for Emotional Regulation

Emotional acceptance

A natural response to feeling sad, afraid and/or ashamed is to try and reject these feelings. However, doing this will likely make it worse. Blocking out an emotion can be an effective strategy if you have the ability to replace it with a more positive emotion. The negative emotions evoked by a teenager in your care need to be actively addressed rather than simply rejected. Failure to address them can lead to feeling compassion fatigue towards the teenager in your care. As a result, you lose empathy for them. Compassion fatigue is comprehensively explored in a later chapter of the book.

Failure to accept an emotion that seems overwhelming often results in the individual turning to other strategies, which can include ambivalent behaviours. For instance, individuals may resort to drinking excessive amounts of alcohol and/or using illegal substances. An alternative to rejecting your emotions is learning to accept them as your emotional experiences, allowing them to be what they are without judgement. The point to be noted here is that it is not the emotions that can harm you but the things you do to reject them, such as excessive alcohol or drug use. When you do accept your emotion, you will be surprised at how capable you become at managing it. Coming to terms with an emotion will help you look at a situation in a different way.

Therapeutically Parenting Teenagers with Developmental Trauma

Reframing

Reframing is the process of looking at things differently. This technique is often used in therapy and is also referred to as cognitive reframing. The idea is to get the person struggling with their emotions to look at things from a different perspective. Individuals feeling 'trapped' in a situation of negativity will probably require a therapist to support them in this process. However, some individuals feel that it is an exercise they can do at home. The fundamental idea is that individuals struggling with their emotions see things through a fixed frame that determines their point of view. When that frame is moved, the meaning attributed to the situation changes; consequently, the individual's thoughts and behaviour often change along with it.

Distress tolerance

Distress tolerance is a person's ability to manage actual or perceived emotional distress. The aim is to get through the feeling without making it any worse. People who have low distress tolerance levels tend to feel overwhelmed by stressful situations, which can lead to disruptive behaviour such as self-harm.

We all experience a variety of stresses during our lifetime. The levels of stress can vary based on the event, ranging from daily annoyances like a bus arriving late to major life changes like losing a loved one or unemployment. Regardless of the level of stress you are coping with, the prime factor here is your ability to tolerate distress – this will have a major impact on how you manage the situation. Learning distress tolerance skills makes a big difference in one's ability to handle difficult emotions (Tull, 2020).

There are a number of distress tolerance techniques that you may find helpful, such as the following:

- Distraction: Distracting yourself is a good way of increasing your distress tolerance, and a variety of methods can be used to take your mind off the feeling of distress. For example, count your breaths: Inhale and exhale, counting it as one, and then inhale and exhale again, counting it as two. Continue counting each cycle of inhalation and exhalation until you reach ten. If you lose count, restart from one.

- Improving the moment: This involves a range of strategies for making stressful situations more tolerable. Some examples are visualising a happy place, doing something pleasant, walking to somewhere nice and listening to some uplifting music.

- Pros and cons: Weigh the pros and cons of tolerating or not tolerating the distress. This will help you focus on the causes and effects of any potential actions.

- Self-soothing: A prime factor of building distress tolerance is finding ways to stay calm and keep negative emotions in check. Different experiences that involve sight, sound, smell, taste or touch can be harnessed to self-soothe during challenging moments.

The goal of distress tolerance is to become more aware of how your emotions influence your responses to distressing situations. We can see how all of the above strategies will work for both the therapeutic parent and the teenager struggling with their emotions.

Communication skills

Communicating your feelings and emotions to yourself and others is an important part of regulating your emotions. To do this, you need to be able to name the emotion; this is linked to emotional awareness. Regulating your emotions and those of the child in your care is an especially important element of therapeutic parenting. Communication is discussed in more detail in later chapters.

Motivation

Motivation is the process that initiates, guides and maintains our goal-oriented behaviours. It is responsible for why you act in certain ways, whether it is going to the fridge to get some food to ease your hunger or reading a book to gain knowledge.

Motivation is driven by the biological, emotional, social and cognitive forces that activate one's behaviour. Often referred to as 'self-motivation', it is used to explain why an individual engages in certain behaviours. You can actually say that it is the driver behind all human actions. However, there is more to motivation than meets the eye. For example, it is not only the factor that activates behaviour; it also involves the factors that maintain and keep on track one's goal-orientated actions. It is exceedingly difficult to identify what factors lie behind an individual's motivation for they are not observable; therefore, you often have to guess why people do certain things.

For many years now, psychologists have been trying to discover why individuals act in certain ways and what exactly lies behind their motivations. The reality is that there are many different forces that guide and direct our motivations.

Different Types of Motivation

Two types of motivation are usually identified when exploring emotional intelligence: intrinsic and extrinsic.

Intrinsic motivation

This is when you participate in a behaviour because you find it worthwhile. You perform an activity for its own sake rather than for any external reward such as money. Intrinsic motivation is an especially important emotional intelligence skill, and people who are skilled in this area are very action orientated. They are motivated by the enjoyment they gain from undertaking the activity and/or their strong belief in or passion for it. In a sense, they have the passion to fulfil their own needs and goals. Individuals who are intrinsically motivated become fully immersed in the activity – time flows, and all of their movements seem to be synchronised, leading to peak performance. This state of mind is referred to as the flow. This approach is usually connected to creative pastimes and sports. However, I believe that the same can apply to learning a new skill, such as therapeutic parenting. When intrinsically motivated, you believe in what you want to achieve and are in tune with your goals, so challenging behaviour rarely fazes you.

The major benefit of being in a state of flow is that it makes the task more enjoyable and achievable. Its other advantages are that it enables better emotional regulation and a greater sense of fulfilment. This then facilitates increased engagement and a hunger to learn more, leading to substantial mastering of the new skill. This also applies to therapeutic parenting. Undertaking a therapeutic approach activity is intrinsically more rewarding. Though clear goals may be challenging, they are still attainable. Knowing that the task is doable creates a balance between the required skill level and the challenge presented. You fully focus on the way you want to parent, i.e. on the strategies you need to apply and the desired outcomes. This will make you feel more in control. The positive response you receive from your therapeutic intervention is the impact this has on the teenager in your care.

Extrinsic motivation

This type of motivation is based on receiving external rewards such as fame, money and praise. Unlike intrinsic motivation, which comes from within, extrinsic motivation comes from factors outside the individual. Think about going to the swimming pool with your friend. If you go to beat them in a contest of who can swim the farthest, your motivation is based on an external reward (here, bragging rights) and, therefore, extrinsic. However, if you go to the swimming pool to have fun and enjoy your time with your friend, your motivation comes from within and is intrinsic.

There are two types of external rewards in extrinsic motivation. These are tangible and psychological rewards. Tangible rewards refer to money and/or trophies. A good example of this can be work. Not everyone enjoys their job, but they still work to earn a wage. Athletes have to undergo torturous training schedules to get to the top of their game and win trophies and/or awards.

Psychological forms of extrinsic motivation involve praise and/or public acclaim. Teenagers might clean their rooms to be praised by their parents and avoid getting into trouble. Actors take up roles to obtain attention and praise from the audience. While these rewards are not physical or tangible, they are motivating for they are external to the actual process of participating in the event.

Extrinsic motivation can and usually is highly effective in certain situations. Take a few minutes to write down some of the things you do to gain some type of external reward. For example, you may shop at the same supermarket so that, after paying for your groceries, you may use your store loyalty card to gain points, which get you discounts on store items; you may undertake boring activities at work to receive your pay check or fly with a specific company to acquire airline miles. All of these activities are extrinsically motivated, and the external rewards make each of the tasks a little more bearable.

Extrinsic motivation is not always a bad thing. External rewards are a useful method of keeping people on the task, especially when it involves activities that the majority of the people find uninteresting, for example, housework or tedious work-related activities.

A word of warning though, extrinsic motivation can backfire. As highlighted, rewards can increase motivation in certain situations, but excessive rewards can and often do lead to a reduction in intrinsic motivation. This is because individuals often analyse their own motivations for engaging in an activity. Once they are rewarded externally for performing an action, they tend to focus more on the reward than on the actual activity. A good example of this is the writing of this book. I love teaching and sharing the knowledge I have by speaking at conferences or writing books. Neither of these activities give me any real external rewards apart from a good book review or a nice comment after a conference. Unless you write a potential bestseller, you are more likely to self-publish a book out of pocket. I personally love writing, and since the first pandemic lockdown, I have managed to write two books about crown green bowling. Writing this current book took up the majority of my time during the third lockdown. Without doubt, my motivation for writing is intrinsic. For me, there are not many things that can surpass the feeling of holding your bound, printed, finished book in your hand for the first time.

The same applies to therapeutic parenting: If your motivation for practising it is extrinsic, your success and motivation will be short-lived! However, if you are intrinsically motivated to give the teenager in your life a really positive trauma-informed parental experience, I have no doubt that you will have an amazing journey.

Empathy

I have already touched upon empathy earlier on in the book when talking about how teenagers who experienced trauma find it exceedingly difficult to show empathy for they probably did not have many opportunities to learn it from adults. Due to their past ACEs, they have more than likely shut down their own feelings as a way of coping. This does have an impact on their ability to develop the skill of empathy. When discussing the application of Dan Hughes's PACE model, I explained that showing empathy lets your teenagers know that you feel compassion for them and that you want to try and understand how they are feeling. By being empathetic, you actively show them that their inner emotions, feelings and experiences are of utmost importance to you.

Empathy, or the ability to understand how others are feeling, is absolutely critical to emotional intelligence. However, it involves more than just being able to recognise the emotional states of others. Empathy entails emotionally understanding how others are feeling, seeing things from their point of view and imagining yourself in their place. Essentially, it is putting yourself in someone else's position and 'walking a mile in their shoes'. You can then respond appropriately based on the information you have acquired. You might treat them with extra care and concern or try to lift their spirits.

While people are generally well attuned to their own feelings and emotions, reading others can be a challenge. For most individuals, responding with disinterest or even absolute hostility to a person in pain is totally unfathomable. But the fact that some people do respond in such a way clearly shows that empathy is not essentially a common response to the suffering and distress of others. You often start to develop your empathy for others at an early age. You are socialised by your parents, peers, local communities and society in general to be predisposed to sympathy, empathy and compassion. How individuals act and feel about others is often based on the beliefs and values they were taught at an incredibly young age (Carpenter, 2020).

To help you identify how empathetic you are as a person, the next section discusses a few signs of empathy.

Signs of Empathy

- You are good at actively listening to what others have to say.

- People often tell you about their problems.
- You are good at picking up on how other people are feeling.
- You often think about how other people feel.
- Other people come to you for advice.
- You often feel overwhelmed by tragic events.
- You try to help others who are suffering.
- You are good at telling when people are not being honest.
- You sometimes feel drained or overwhelmed in social situations.
- You care deeply about other people.
- You find it difficult to set boundaries in your relationships with other people. (Kendra, 2020)

Having lots of empathy and caring for a teenager with developmental trauma makes you susceptible to burnout or even overstimulation due to the constant consideration of someone else's emotions. This is referred to as compassion fatigue, which is discussed in detail later on in the book.

There is no doubt that you benefit by being empathetic. Empathy allows you to build social connections with other people, and research has shown that social connections are important for your physical and psychological wellbeing. Understanding what other people are feeling and thinking enables you to respond appropriately in social environments. Empathising also teaches you how to regulate your own emotions, which is especially important for emotional intelligence and when supporting teenagers with developmental trauma. Showing empathy to your teenager will also enable them to feel empathy for others.

Lack of Empathy

Some people are naturally more empathetic than others. Some will feel more empathy towards certain people and less towards others. This can be influenced by past experiences and expectations, how one perceives the other person, what blame they attach to the other person's behaviours, and what they think has informed the other person's situation.

There can be a few different explanations for why some people lack empathy. Most often, people lack empathy due to the way they perceive the world around them. For example, they may attribute other people's failures to their internal characteristics, while blaming their own situation on external factors. Being unable to see all the factors that contribute to a situation means that they are less likely to be able to see a situation from the perspective of others. This is referred to as cognitive bias (Loftus, 1988).

Another reason can be that the individual perceives some people as 'different' due to differing actions and behaviours. Said individual then dehumanises the situation. For example, an individual who sees a report on TV about a natural disaster in a far-off place may be less likely to feel empathy for the victims, perceiving the people who are suffering as profoundly different from themselves.

I previously raised the point that children and teenagers who have underwent ACEs and are living with developmental trauma are not able to feel empathy. This is because they could not learn it from their parents and because they have more than likely suppressed their own feelings as a means of protection. The right level of support and nurturing and actually experiencing empathy will give them the opportunity to develop the empathetic pathways in their brain.

Tips for Practising and Developing Empathy

Empathy is a skill that you can learn, strengthen and help others develop. Start off by practising the following basic exercises, and you should see an improvement in a noticeably short period of time. Practise listening to other people without interrupting them. Do take notice of body language and other types of non-verbal communication for they play a particularly important role when we try to read other's emotions and feelings. Take a 'step back', and do try to understand other people, even if you do not agree with them. I have previously discussed creative visualisation as a tool for facilitating and enhancing your mind training. Visualisation can also be used when trying to enhance your empathy skills. Building empathy into your visualisations will not only make them more realistic but also embed empathy into your subconscious. Empathy is such an important aspect of both emotional intelligence and therapeutic parenting. The need to put time and energy into developing your empathy skills cannot be overemphasised.

Social Skills

Being able to interact with and engage others well is another important aspect of emotional intelligence. Having strong social skills allows individuals to build meaningful relationships with other people while developing a stronger understanding of themselves and others.

Emotional understanding involves more than just understanding your own and others' emotions; you also need to be able to use this information in your daily interactions and communications, for example, when working with other professionals such as social workers, teachers, therapists, fellow carers, etc. It goes without saying that having the ability to develop a strong rapport with the teenager in your care is priceless. To effectively build rapport, you will have to develop a strong set of social skills, which include active listening, verbal communication, non-verbal communication and negotiation skills. I am sure that you recognise that all of these skills are also connected to therapeutic parenting.

Individuals with social intelligence can sense how other people feel, know intuitively what to say in social situations and seem self-assured even when all eyes are on them. With regard to parenting, they seem to be able to read situations and act accordingly. In a sense, it seems like they have a presence without even saying anything. You will often hear others saying that such individuals have 'people skills', but what they truly possess is a set of well-developed social skills that make them socially intelligent.

Core Traits of Social Intelligence

Described below are the core traits associated with social intelligence that help a socially apt individual connect and communicate effectively with others:

Effective listening

People who possess social intelligence do not listen merely to respond. They give their undivided attention when they are being spoken to. This is really important when parenting. For example, playing on your phone or answering a text message must never take precedence over active listening. When your teenagers speak to you, stop what you are doing and listen to them. The aim here is to ensure that, when they walk away, they feel that they were listened to and understood and that they made a connection.

Conversational skills

Have you ever seen someone 'work the room'? They have conversational skills that enable them to carry on a discussion with practically everybody in the room. They seem to have the skill to change their conversation tone from thoughtful to appropriately witty or sincere as they handle a wide range of conversation topics and a large number of people. They seem to be able to remember things about people whom they have not seen for some time. This shows that a good skill to master is remembering little details about people; when you meet them again in the future, you can use the information as an icebreaker, putting you both at ease. For example, suppose that a person's dog had just returned from the vet the last time you talked to them. Remembering this detail the next time you see them and asking about their dog will automatically reconnect you. This principle applies to young people too. When your teenager brings friends home and you have previously met them, remembering little things such as the music they like, if they have a pet, what their hobbies are, etc., will help break the ice. I am not proposing that you refine your social intelligence skills to such a level that you become able to 'work a room', but we all can observe and learn from individuals who can do so.

Reputation management

Socially intelligent people think about the impression that they make on other people. However, managing a reputation is a precarious balancing act. It is important to think carefully about the kind of impression you create – your aim must be to remain authentic. With regard to working with and parenting teenagers, you must never collude with them in their behaviours, especially harmful ones, as a means of being accepted. Just be yourself; if you are a warm, caring and fun individual, why would they not like you?

Lack of arguing

People with social intelligence understand that by arguing or proving a point while making another person or teenager feel bad or ashamed, they achieve nothing in the long term. Even though you may not agree with the point that the teenager is making, never reject any of their ideas outright. What you need to do is listen to them with an open mind even if you do not agree with their idea. Even when they are being racist, sexist and/or homophobic, you should listen to them and then supportively challenge the point they are making. Simply jumping down a young person's throat when they put forward a discriminatory point will not resolve the issue. It is better to listen and then respond in a calm tone to what they are saying. Arguing should not be a part of any therapeutic parenting approach for it results in nothing but shame.

Many people develop social intelligence without really trying, while others have to work to develop it. Below are a few strategies that may help you build and/or enhance your social intelligence:

How to Develop Social Intelligence

Pay close attention to what (and who) is around you

Socially intelligent people are observant and pay attention to subtle social cues from those around them. My advice to you is that when you are out and about, undertake a little 'people watching'; you can learn so much from observing others. Also, I believe that observing others undertake a therapeutic parenting approach is a great training tool. If you think that someone in your life has strong people skills, watch how they interact with others. Trust me, you can learn so much.

Work on increasing your emotional intelligence

Although similar to social intelligence, emotional intelligence is more about how you control your own emotions and how you empathise with others. It involves recognising your emotions and understanding, interpreting and responding to the emotions of others, thereby regulating them appropriately. An emotionally intelligent person can identify and control negative feelings, such as frustration or anger, when in a challenging situation. This is why I personally feel that emotional intelligence is key if you want to parent therapeutically.

Respect cultural differences

A large number of us learn our social skills from our families, friends and the wider community. It is worthwhile considering this when you observe the social skills in your teenagers for they have more than likely come from a very chaotic and challenging background. The issue is that when you are developing your own social skills, you have to be aware of any cultural differences. Do not shy away from this; I recommend proactively seeking out different cultures so that you can gain a better understanding. A socially intelligent person understands that others might have different responses and customs based on their upbringing.

Practise active listening

An especially important component of social awareness is active listening. Here are a few golden rules that you should try to embed into your communication skills; these are also essential when working with teenagers with developmental trauma: Take time to think about what someone else is saying before you respond. Listen to their tone as it can give you clues about what they are trying to communicate – look behind their words.

Active listening enables you to develop and build relationships. It allows you to understand the other person's point of view and respond with empathy. It also allows you to ask for clarification in an unthreatening way and make sure that you understand what is being said.

Being an active listener in a discussion demonstrates that you recognise that the conversation is more about the other person than about yourself. This is especially important when the other person is distressed. This enables you to become an empathetic listener, who we all need at certain times in our lives.

The ability to listen to a distraught friend or teenager is a valuable skill. Active listening will stop you from acting on the urge to jump in with a 'quick fix' when what the other person needs is just to be heard. They are not in a position to listen to strategies and/or take advice. Active listening will make them feel validated and encourage them to speak longer. You can see how valuable this approach could be when talking with a distraught teenager.

Be aware of non-verbal communication

Non-verbal communication helps reinforce or adapt what is being said while also conveying information about an individual's emotional state. An example of this could be when someone shrugs their shoulders when responding, 'I'm fine, thanks'. This actually implies that things are not fine at all!

An individual's tone of voice, facial expression and body posture can tell others exactly how they are feeling even if they hardly say a word. Non-verbal communication can give you an insight into what is going on with your teenager. It can and often does define the relationship between two people; they actually start to mirror each other's movements and gestures. For example, they hold their hands in similar positions, smile in unison and will turn to face each other more fully. This can be a clear indication that they are starting to develop a rapport, which leads to a real positive connection. Connections are really important if you are going to support a teenager through trauma. This is covered in more detail later on in the book.

Non-verbal communication also acts as a positive feedback for the other person. Smiles and nods inform them that you are listening and that you agree with what they are saying. Movement and hand gestures can indicate that you wish to speak. These slight signals give information gently but clearly. You can use a number of signals to tell people that you have finished speaking or that you wish to speak. An obvious nod and firm closing of the lips indicate that you have finished speaking. Making eye contact at a meeting and nodding slightly will indicate that you wish to speak. Non-verbal communication, in a sense, regulates the flow of a conversation. Reading non-verbal behaviours is an important element of therapeutic parenting.

A word of warning here: Interpreting non-verbal communication is not always straightforward; it can be both conscious and unconscious. Facial expressions can actually form without you knowing about it. You may be trying to communicate one message consciously while conveying quite another unconsciously.

I hope that this section on social intelligence, an important component of social skills, and emotional intelligence has been of some benefit to you in your quest to be a therapeutic parent. Social intelligence does take some mastering, but it is so important when trying to build a relationship with a teenager living with developmental trauma. I do hope that some of the above strategies have given you the confidence to explore them in more depth. Give them a try, and be prepared to learn from your successes and failures as both are equally important.

Conclusion

We can see what an important component emotional intelligence is with regard to training one's mind. When it is coupled with the other aspects of goal setting, dealing with self-doubt, affirmation and creative visualisation, our aim of embedding a new way of thinking and responding into our subconscious mind becomes a distinct possibility.

Emotionally intelligent people know that while emotions can be powerful, they are temporary. When a highly charged emotional event takes place, such as being confronted with challenging behaviour from a teenager, the emotionally intelligent response would be to take some time before responding. This allows parents to calm their emotions and think more rationally about all the factors surrounding the argument: What is behind this behaviour? What is our teenager trying to communicate?

Emotionally intelligent people are not only good at thinking about how other people might feel but also adept at understanding their own feelings. Being self-aware about their emotions allows them to consider the many different factors that contribute to their emotions. They also have the ability to self-regulate their own emotions and those of others.

A large part of emotional intelligence is being able to think about and empathise with how other people are feeling. This often involves considering how you would respond if you were in the same situation. Knowing what motivates you to become a therapeutic parent is the start of the journey. Being socially intelligent will also benefit your interactions in a wide range of settings and be beneficial for your relationship with the teenager in your care.

Having strong emotional intelligence will enable you to consider the perspectives, experiences and emotions of other people and use this information to explain why they are behaving the way they are. This, in turn, enables you to think and respond therapeutically. I previously identified the need to retrain your subconscious mind if you are going to make the transition from a standard parenting style to a therapeutic one. You want your subconscious mind to be able to filter challenging behaviours and routinely seek out therapeutic responses, informed by the learnt methods and strategies that underpin therapeutic parenting. I did acknowledge that this is not an easy task. However, I hope that this in-depth section on training your mind to think and respond differently will be of help. Remember that this is a marathon, not a sprint. It will take time and great effort on your part. However, the changes in your teenager when you apply a therapeutic parenting style will be immense, making the effort more than worthwhile.

PARENTING YOUR TEENAGERS

Chapter 9:

COMMUNICATING WITH A TEENAGER WITH DEVELOPMENTAL TRAUMA

I have explored in depth how teenagers who undergo ACEs often go on to develop emotional and behavioural difficulties. The trauma impacts their brain development, and they are often said to have developmental trauma. Their behaviour will make them seem to have anger issues and project them as rude, defiant and extremely ignorant. We know that many of the behaviours that we see and identify in our teenagers are fear-based responses stemming from how their brains have developed. It is highly likely that they lack self-esteem and are not confident in communicating their needs.

When teenagers join your family, you can expect that they will be hypervigilant to keep themselves safe. They will also have trouble regulating their emotions and, without doubt, have major trust issues. They will likely try to manage their fear and anxiety by attempting to control their environment and the people around them. Abuse, neglect and trauma shape teenagers' internal working models in such a way that they do not feel good enough for or worthy of good things or even love and affection. This is rooted in both their conscious and subconscious mind. They will also feel ashamed, and you can expect them to not have had the opportunity to develop empathy skills. Your challenge will be to try to develop a rapport with them; there does need to be some form of connection before you can effectively start the process of therapeutically parenting them (Siegel, 2012).

Setting the Scene

So, how do you go about breaking the ice? What you need to do is try and create a relaxed family atmosphere without putting them under any pressure to interact. A positive family environment is really important for children and young people who have experienced trauma, as they need to live in a safe and nurturing home that allows them to experience mutual enjoyment, respect and opportunities (Golding, 2008). This is discussed in more detail when covering family life in Chapter 11. This is an especially important component for enabling communication; without the right family environment, you cannot create an empathetic, nurturing safe space that facilitates healing.

Initiating some banter can help build an initial relationship, which the teenager will, hopefully, feel is worth investing in. The brief exchanges that take place while watching television or as all family members go about their business will help them feel settled and give them the confidence to join in discussions. All this helps in breaking the ice and setting the scene for how the family members interact in a safe and secure environment.

A relaxed environment often makes the teenagers want to talk about their past experiences; at this stage, they are testing you out to see your reaction. This is where PACE and other strategies come into play. However, it is important that you let the young person raise these issues and lead the discussion. When establishing a relationship, a balance should be maintained between banter and seriousness as and when required. Doing this is not easy, and the process is difficult to put into words. A lot of it is based on intuition and how you are as a person. There is value in discussing with the teenagers why they think, act and process things the way they do. Obviously, you should not overcomplicate the issue; just use a basic explanation. This then enables them to have some self-awareness, which is an important component of self-regulation. Explaining these issues in a non-judgemental way with an appropriate level of humour and playfulness goes a long way in cementing your relationship with the teenager in your care. When you have been through a challenging situation together, do reflect on their behaviour at a later date when they are in a 'good place'. Do not dwell on it, but ensure that you get to name your own emotions and theirs. Take every effort to reinforce your presence without being overbearing. For example, if they have been out of the home for a long period of time, do send them a text; if they have been in their room most of the evening, do check in on them. Definitely make a conscientious effort to make time for your teenager, regardless of how busy you are. It is really important to accept them for who they are and your place in their world. Knowing this is an excellent starting point for building a solid foundation for a positively attuned relationship.

Attunement

I have discussed the need to create a connection with the teenagers in your care. The most productive approach for achieving this is creating an environment that is both nurturing and empathetic for this will lead to emotional attunement. You may recall that we touched upon attunement while exploring PACE and identified that it is how an individual reacts to another person. Teenagers who feel that they have a connection with an adult who is consistent and provides balanced reactions to their communication and needs are more likely to want to engage in conversation. An attuned response enables the teenagers to feel understood and not judged, as has been explored in the section about PACE. Attunement actually allows you to share emotions with your teenager.

Non-Verbal Communication

You may recall that when I discussed emotional intelligence, I outlined the importance of non-verbal communication in social intelligence. The ability to understand the non-verbal cues by your teenager is crucial if you wish to connect with them emotionally. More often than not, it is non-verbal communication that really expresses what the teenager is feeling. You also have to be aware of your own non-verbal cues as your tone of voice, eye contact, facial expressions and touch convey that you have a level of understanding. Teenagers who live with developmental trauma find it extremely difficult to even make sense of their own emotions and feelings, let alone verbalise them (Golding, 2008).

Below, I have included a few tips on how to deal with situations in which even though things are not going so well, you need to keep the communication channels open. There will be times when you will have to talk seriously with them about certain issues affecting the household, which could potentially result in them getting upset or angry. How can you make sure that your conversation is effective and really changes things without destroying your relationship?

Dealing with difficult discussions

Timing is everything. Never try to address issues when either one or both of you are tired. Do not go jumping on your teenagers as they walk through the door or they will probably slam it in your face. Choose your time and place. More importantly, make sure that you are calm, and if they tell you from the outset that they do not want to talk about this now, respect their wishes. However, try and negotiate a time for rescheduling the discussion.

Have clear and concise boundaries in relation to your expectations. Think carefully about what you expect – What is your goal? Be assertive and consistent, but be open to negotiations; more importantly, be flexible. Ensure that you strike a balance between keeping them safe and allowing them some independence. They need to be able to learn from their own mistakes, which will enable them to develop risk assessment skills.

Try to avoid being defensive, and never take things personally. It is highly likely that they are not angry with you. You are just in the wrong place at the wrong time. Never collude with your teenager for it has no benefit whatsoever. What you are striving for is a relationship based on a level playing field.

Negotiation is an especially important skill in life. Show your teenagers how to negotiate, present their point of view respectfully and come to an agreement. Use every opportunity to teach them this skill within the family unit. Further, listen to your teenager; let them speak. Whether you agree with their point of view is irrelevant. Make sure to use 'active listening' so that they know you are giving them your full attention. Start from a position of understanding when responding to them. Agreeing is not the issue here; showing respect for their opinions is. Be specific, and stay focused. Never go off on a tangent and bring other issues into the discussion. Take one issue at a time, stay focused and be assertive when you have to, but also be aware of your tone. This is a discussion, not a lecture. Ensure that they also feel that they are a participant and have a view.

When you feel angry, stressed, upset and/or let down, try to share this with your teenagers, but choose the correct language so as to not inflict shame. Do not make any accusations; be respectful, and be aware of your tone.

This also applies to when you know that they are about to do something that you do not agree with. Think carefully about how you will deal with this; ask yourself if it is worth getting upset and angry about. Could you approach this in another way? How can you avoid unnecessary conflict?

Try to keep your own emotions regulated. However, if you feel that you are struggling with this in a discussion, ask to take some time out. Explain that you need to calm down before you try to put your point across in a way that does not make either of you emotional or angry. The response you get may not be what you want, but it is still a good skill to share (Holland, 2020).

When you do get angry (for you are only human) or react in a way that you are not happy with, it is important to repair the situation. Choose the right moment and apologise. Modelling repair is good for our teenagers. I never expect them to say sorry to me, but I am more than willing to say sorry myself.

My last point is in relation to taking advantage of some of the TV dramas that young people like to watch. Taking out some time to sit and watch these with them does give you a great opportunity to explore sensitive issues from a third person's perspective. They can feel free to comment and share their views without personalising their responses. This can be a powerful method to enable them to be open and honest and not fear shame or reprisal.

Conclusion

The most important element of therapeutic parenting is the relationship that you have or are trying to develop with the teenager in your care. Getting them to invest in a relationship with you is never easy. However, by being patient, giving them time and, most importantly, accepting them for who they are, you can make it happen. This will encourage meaningful communication, which will, in turn, allow you to start a therapeutic intervention. Teenagers living with developmental trauma have to deal with so many emotions on a daily basis. Therefore, someone who can give them the time and an empathetic ear without judgement is what they need. Only then can they start making sense of their world.

Chapter 10:
DEVELOPING RESILIENCE IN YOUR TEENAGER

I previously explained how emotional intelligence is an intricate part of mind training and therapeutic parenting. I actually believe that if you want to help the teenager in your care build resilience, you need to have a high level of emotional intelligence. The purpose of this chapter is to identify some of the protective factors that are required to enable a teenager living with trauma to build resilience. It is important to acknowledge that resilience is not about pushing through, taking control or carrying on regardless of how you feel; it is about developing strategies that help you manage stressful situations.

We all respond to stressful situations differently. Maybe you're someone who can carry on without a second thought, or perhaps you are someone who finds quite minor difficulties overwhelming. Having the ability to respond positively and learn from stressful situations is what we call resilience. A good way to define resilience is the ability one has to cope with and/or recover from stressful and even traumatic experiences. Research has acknowledged that children and teenagers with secure attachments that led to positive internal working models do have all the protective factors that contribute towards the building of resilience (Moore, 2020). However, for teenagers with disorganised internal working models that result in their feeling worthless and undeserving of positive experiences, building resilience is difficult. This is because struggling with one's relationships, feelings and/or past experiences does have a major impact on the development of resilience.

Resilience is developed through a series of interactions between a teenager's ACEs and protective factors. The quality of interactions is what determines the development of a teenager. Positive interactions will enable the teenager to build resilience, which should lead to positive wellbeing. Similarly, negative interactions will more than likely result in low resilience, leading to illness and dysfunction.

Teenagers are not going to suddenly wake up one morning and find that they are magically resilient to the impact of their ACEs, just as no teenager is automatically doomed due to ACEs. The presence of protective factors, particularly safe, stable and nurturing relationships, can alleviate the consequences of ACEs. Individuals, families and communities can all influence the development of many protective factors throughout a teenager's life, which can impact his or her development.

How does resilience develop? There are multiple pathways to resilience, and you have a major role to play in them all as the parent or caregiver.

Close Relationships with Caring Adults within a Family Unit

With the support of a competent caregiver, teenagers will start being more aware of their emotions and even regulating them. They will become more self-aware. They will be able to explore their trauma and previous ACEs in a caring, nurturing and non-judgemental environment. They should also gain positive insights into family life with well-defined roles, boundaries and clear responsibilities.

Therapeutically Parenting Teenagers with Developmental Trauma

Parent Resilience

The more emotionally intelligent you become, the more resilient you will be as a therapeutic parent. You will also understand the need to look after yourself. Taking care of yourself will enable you to provide your teenager with consistent, nurturing and empathetic care. Challenging situations will become less stressful, and you will be able to build a better connection with the teenager in your care.

Caregiver Knowledge and Application of Positive Parenting Skills

I have covered in depth the need for parents to understand the type of parenting a teenager with developmental trauma needs (see Chapter 3). Parenting teenagers with developmental trauma is not an easy task, but it is a rewarding one. Helping young people build resilience against their trauma by providing them with a number of protective factors not only makes them more stable but also supports them in working towards independence.

Identifying and Cultivating a Sense of Purpose Through the Development of Individual Factors

If the necessary support and protective factors are in place, teenagers will start to develop a feeling of control over their lives. Having a close relationship with caring adults will help develop in them a sense of cohesion with others and, hopefully, a sense of humour. Rather than seeking out immediate gratification, they should be able to build up tolerance for delayed fulfilment. They should also be given opportunities to learn how to deal with criticism, rejection and silence. Self-regulating their emotions will also enable them to develop problem-solving skills. Slowly but surely, their internal working model will start to change to form a positive sense of self.

Social Connections

Participating in school, work, community groups, sport clubs and/or simply having a small friendship group will give them a sense of belonging in the world and make them feel as though they are contributing to it. Having a social network will aid them in developing and maintaining friendships. Hopefully, after becoming more resilient, they will no longer feel the need to control or be controlled by their peers to feel safe. Social connections are particularly important because teenagers need to feel able and confident enough to function not only within a family setting but also in the wider community.

Conclusion

Protective factors help a teenager feel safe relatively soon after experiencing the toxic stress of ACEs. The more protective factors available to a teenager when they are feeling the impact of toxic stress, the more capacity they have to develop resilience.

The negative consequences of ACEs can be counteracted with support, care and appropriate interventions. Through positive relationships, teenagers learn to develop crucial coping skills. They know that they are not alone, and they adopt healthy ways to process stress.

When teenagers are taught coping mechanisms, they start to exercise their resilience muscle. They need to keep practising resilience (training their resilience muscle) for this enables them to continue growing stronger, making them better equipped to manage the ups and downs of life.

Resilience building does not happen overnight, and unless the necessary protective factors are in place, this is unlikely to happen. Through the process of therapeutic parenting, you can not only help the teenagers in your life deal with their trauma but also, more importantly, play a major, instrumental role in them living life to their full potential.

Chapter 11:
FAMILY LIFE

Central to creating a positive family atmosphere is your learning to stay calm and in control of your behaviour and emotions. We have explored in detail the need to support teenagers in self-regulation, but you may also recall that your own self-regulation is an especially important part of emotional intelligence and therapeutic parenting. Staying self-regulated will also create a calm atmosphere in the home. This is so important if you want the teenager to feel safe and start to heal and develop. You might not be able to control your teenager's behaviour for you can only respond to it therapeutically, which entails having clear boundaries underpinned by empathy and nurturing. However, you do have to take responsibility for your own behaviour and actions.

What is a Family Atmosphere?

The importance of creating a family atmosphere was brought up in the chapter about communicating with a teenager with developmental trauma. It was identified that to create a connection with you, teenagers need to be in an environment where they can experience mutual enjoyment, have fun, feel respected and have the opportunity to develop and start building resilience.

It is important to establish clear boundaries and structures that help facilitate consistency for creating such an atmosphere. Doing so will lead to a reduction in challenging behaviours as the teenager's feelings of safety and security will increase. Being in a family atmosphere that allows them to experience empathy, nurturing and love will also enable them to experience and explore feelings of trust and wellbeing.

Unfortunately, it is highly likely that their past experiences of family life were quite different from the one you are trying to create in your home. They may have been forced to learn to live in a totally different atmosphere, one full of hostility, tension, rage, fear and long periods of isolation. It is very doubtful that there were set mealtimes, and any boundaries must have been very chaotic or non-existent. Any similar experiences in your home will trigger memories of their previous family. They will feel at home even so, having developed coping strategies to survive in such environments. However, this will confirm their fear that what they believe about themselves and others is true; this is essentially a confirmation of what their internal working model believes. Some teenagers will find it extremely difficult to adapt and settle in a calm family environment. Therefore, they will do their utmost to recreate the environment they are used to, an environment full of hostility and tension. As a result, their fear and anxiety will return, which is not conducive to their healing. You will also see them return to their challenging behaviours as a way of surviving.

Creating the family atmosphere before the teenagers join a family is relatively easy. However, maintaining it will be very challenging. What you need to take into consideration is that the teenager is leaving a totally different environment, one that was very chaotic and that forced them to learn how to live with fear and constant disruption. Therefore, they will find it exceedingly difficult to settle in an environment that is totally alien to them. Therefore, it is likely that setting a stable routine will increase their anxiety levels. This may result in them asking you many questions: 'Why do I have to go to bed at 10 PM? Why do we have to sit at the table together to eat meals? Why are you not shouting at me or hitting me? Why do I have to be home by 9.30 PM?' The teenager will more than likely push against all the boundaries you set. What you must do is offer them lots of support to lower the anxiety they are feeling while adapting to an environment that is totally different from what they are used to. You must also apply all the principles of therapeutic parenting, have lots of patience and access support for yourself as and when required.

Points to Consider

Kim Golding (2008) highlighted the following principles for supporting a child in fitting into a new family and included some tips for maintaining the family atmosphere:

Do apply empathy and playfulness and keep your tone calm for this will help you maintain empathy for and be accepting of your teenagers while they are adjusting to their new environment. The benefit here can be twofold as speaking calmly and soothingly to an angry teenager (extrinsic) can actually decrease your own anger (intrinsic). You may recall that we covered this when we discussed using playfulness to regulate not only the teenagers but also ourselves.

Creating the expectation that they will adjust to the new family environment and having clear boundaries and rules in place will facilitate the process of their settling in. It is important that you have a non-intrusive, matter-of-fact attitude as being critical, harsh and complaining will only send the teenagers closer to their original experiences, which will make it less likely that they will successfully make the transition.

You must ensure that boundaries and structures are maintained and any breaking of these result in natural, logical consequences. However, when setting these, be sure to undertake the three Rs approach: Make sure that they are related, respectable and reasonable and delivered with empathy and lots of support.

Even when the teenager is not following boundaries and rules, do keep reassuring them that they will adapt to this new and vastly different environment. Tell them that although they are struggling, you know that they are a great person with a big heart. Making them feel liked and wanted will probably result in their trying to push you away and cause arguments; but remember, by consistently applying the principles of PACE, you can help them regulate their emotions. The golden rule here is to respond to any hostility with empathy and remain calm, interested and patient. Attunement will take time; what you need to do is try to build a rapport with them whenever the situation allows.

What is really important to remember is that you are not a saint; you will have days when you react in a way that is not as empathetic as you would have liked. Do not beat yourself up. You are trying your best, and you can always go and repair your relationship with your teenager, which, for me, is modelling good behaviour. However, before that, take some time out for yourself. You need to relax; go and enjoy for some time with a friend. When you feel rejuvenated, brush yourself down and get ready to go at it again.

Additional Information for Families to Consider

The term 'family' probably means different things to different people. For some individuals, the term describes the large gatherings they have four to five times a year. On the other hand, the members of some families live in close proximity to each other, and they are in and out of each other's homes on a daily basis. There are some families that only meet at weddings and/or funerals. I am guessing that for the majority of the families who want to welcome a child or teenager into their family unit to help them recover from trauma and reach their full potential, family is everything.

When it comes to exploring family life, Sally Donovan (2019) highlights some good tips in *The Unofficial Guide to Therapeutic Parenting – The Teen Years*.

While discussing holidays, she explores how a lot of teenagers living with developmental trauma struggle to cope with change. She cautions against going on that dream holiday you have been planning for years for it could end up a disaster. It might be better to save it for when you eventually retire. I agree with her philosophy regarding holidays: short breaks, self-catering with lots to keep the teenagers occupied and no big expectations from you. I would suggest not going too far away from home in case you have to come home early because a family member is struggling. I will also think long and hard before taking abroad a teenager who struggles with self-regulation and suffers from a high degree of anxiety.

Donovan also highlights issues regarding festivities and argues your teenager should be allowed to voice whether they want to participate or not. Many children and young people who are not with their birth families struggle at Christmas for it is usually presented as a joyous family occasion. The same can apply to Father's Day and Mother's Day for they may view it totally differently from how we see it. My advice is to never force a teenager to attend a family function if they do not want to go. If you do, I can foresee that it has 'disaster' written all over it! Once you get to know your teenager, you will be able to anticipate what they can and cannot cope with.

Parenting a traumatised teenager will put stress on your relationship, with other family members and with your circle of friends. I have found that therapeutically parenting a teenager with developmental trauma sorts the chaff from the wheat. Now, I definitely know who among my friends and family I can rely on one-hundred percent. I have to say that my extended family has genuinely accepted our decision to become a fostering family, and my partner and I truly value their support and understanding.

I have written a lot about parenting therapeutically, applying the principles of PACE and underpinning it with emotional intelligence. Regarding the family unit, I have to say that both parents definitely need to sign up for the therapeutic journey. However, a word of warning: Some individuals take to therapeutic parenting quicker than others. You both need to be patient and understanding and support each other in catching up. I would recommend trying to have the same level of understanding for the partner who is struggling as you have for your teenager. Once you are both singing from the same hymn sheet, you will find that your house functions more fluently and is peaceful most of the time (fingers crossed).

I would also recommend that you do reflect on how your family's day went on certain occasions. Be prepared to explore behaviours, what was behind them, what went well and what could have been handled better. Golden rule number one: Remember, you are only human(s), and although what you are doing is really worthwhile, it can also wear you down to the bone if you do not recognise the need for support and/or some time out. Be prepared to give yourself and your other half all the praise and support required. A word here for single carers: Make sure that you have a really good support network – someone you can call at 11 PM to vent and/or share good times with.

Conclusion

Creating a calm family atmosphere is paramount if you wish to create a healing environment for the teenagers in your care. Accept that their experience of family life was quite different from what you are trying to create for them. This will give rise to challenges from the outset. However, by setting clear boundaries and structures underpinned by empathy and nurturing, you will eventually see a reduction in the challenging behaviours. Again, what is important here is to try and understand the reasons behind the behaviour and what your teenager is trying to communicate. Creating the family atmosphere is fairly easy; maintaining it is the hard part. Opening up your family for a new family member will always lead to challenges. What is important is to learn and move forward together. This is a new experience for all the parties involved, but creating a fun-filled, empathetic environment where all family members are nurtured will make the journey so much easier.

Chapter 12:

FRIENDSHIPS

Friendships are incredibly important during adolescence. Teen friendships help young people feel a sense of acceptance and belonging. Teenagers' relationships with their peers support the development of compassion, caring and empathy. Teenage friendships play a big part in the formation of a sense of identity outside the family. Yes, they can be problematic, but having a close network of friends does have a wide range of benefits. Teenagers with a friendship group often feel a sense of belonging; as a result, they have positive feelings about their relationships with other people in society. Teenagers benefit from having good social connections as it equips them with better self-esteem, a more optimistic outlook, stronger emotion regulation skills, improved cognitive function and more empathy and trust towards others.

Dan Siegel (2017) believes that teenagers' desire for friendship is biologically hardwired. It is natural to turn towards peers as a teenager because these are the people you will depend on when you eventually leave home. Siegel sees this as part of learning how to survive.

The social skills that are required to develop and maintain friendships are complex and take time for all children to learn. Thus, for children and young people who experienced trauma, learning social skills can be extremely challenging. Trauma can have a serious impact on children and young people's normal developmental processes, making it difficult for them to understand social cues, regulate emotions well, understand the perspective of others and develop empathy.

Therefore, the impact of trauma on teenagers' development will create difficulties with regard to their capacity to make friends. Research has shown that trauma affects their ability to make decisions and control their impulses. At the same time, trauma can affect teenagers' reactivity to stress and emotional situations. So, teenagers who have experienced trauma may feel the need to control their friends or develop friendship with an individual who controls them. They may also face problems in reacting to situations in which they cannot self-regulate their emotions. This often results in their being left out of groups and friendships breaking up quickly.

Making Poor Friendship Choices

You will find that the teenager in your care often makes bad friendship choices. This is because well-adjusted young people may find them immature, over the top and unpredictable. You are already aware of this and accustomed to it, but, unfortunately, their peers are not. This leaves your teenager with an exceedingly small pool of young people to choose their friends from. You will often find them gravitating towards other young people who are a little wayward and may have problems of their own; they always seem to get into trouble at school, take risks and be allowed out at all hours of the day and night. These types of relationships are not demanding in terms of attachment. They usually consist of a group of similar-minded young people who either choose to use the streets or one of the young people's homes (especially where there is little or no parental supervision) as a recreational resource. Quite often, such groups participate in risk-taking behaviour, and there is a lot of peer pressure; you have to partake in specific activities if you wish to remain a part of the group. Fall outs within the group are a regular occurrence.

The teenager in your care will more than likely go through a large number of short-term friendships, which will make them experience a lot of hurt and rejection. This will then confirm their internal working model that they are not good enough to have friendships. As parents, you will probably find this extremely painful to observe. Your teenager is desperate to be accepted and constantly tell themselves that they are not good enough; this puts them at risk and leaves them extremely vulnerable. Adolescence is the period in which they should be moving away from family and slowly transitioning to a supportive peer group through which they can learn so much about others and themselves. Not having the social skills to participate in this transition will often result in their spending the majority of the day and, if allowed, the entire night on social media.

Technology and Teenage Isolation

When teenagers struggle to form friendships and engage in face-to-face interactions, they often try to substitute real-life connections with virtual ones. As a result, they will find it more comfortable to relate to their peers from the safety of their bedroom via text, Messenger, Facebook, Snapchat and other social networks rather than actual face-to-face conversation. This can put them at risk of becoming a victim of predators who use social media as a way of grooming children so that they can sexually exploit them.

Two studies on smartphone use showed how teenagers are becoming addicted to their smartphones and how the frequency of their social media use has an impact on how they feel. It was found that participants who constantly checked Facebook or other networking sites were more distressed than those who checked them just a few times a day (Underwood, 2015).

Caroline Fenkel (2017) identified in her research that there is a link between smartphone addiction and social isolation. Social withdrawal creates an increased risk of smartphone and social media addiction among adolescents. Research has found that scrolling through a newsfeed and receiving 'likes' on social media activates the same circuits in the teenage brain as eating chocolate or winning money does. Specifically, dopamine is released in the brain. Therefore, frequent use of smartphones and social media actually rewires the developing teen brain to constantly seek out immediate gratification (Pantic, 2014). This can lead to other addictive behaviours. In fact, studies have found that Internet and smart phone addiction have a similar effect on the brain as heroin and other drugs do. One can imagine the impact all of this can have on a teenager's traumatised brain when it is developing.

I have had many discussions and attended training courses where carers expressed their horror at the number of hours their teenagers spent on their Internet devices. They had regularly observed the adrenaline rush their teenagers experienced when falling out with their virtual friends. A number of teenagers actually seek out chat groups that they can join with the sole purpose of being detrimental to each other. The term they use is giving each other 'beef'. You do not need a degree in psychology to see how harmful this can be to teenagers who cannot regulate their emotions and already have a very low opinion of themselves.

Supporting Teenagers in Forming Friendships

The good news is that, even though trauma can affect the developing brain, we know from research that the brain keeps growing and changing for many years throughout childhood and adolescence. This means that you can help your teenager develop their social skills and show them how to develop healthy friendships and maintain them.

Building on Existing Skills

A very important component of developing and maintaining friendships is understanding the role that social skills play in everyday interactions. I personally believe that enabling teenagers with developmental trauma to identify the different social skills is a good starting point for the same. Once they understand and recognise the roles that non-verbal communication, effective and active listening, and dealing with conflict play within relationships, they will be better equipped to develop their own skill base. I have talked a lot about playfulness and the need to be serious when required, and I think that this is a good approach to take when working on social skills. For example, you can develop some fun games related to listening skills or reading others' expressions and even engage in some fun role play. It is important to provide feedback on the skills that you feel your teenager already has as well as the areas that they should develop. I believe that the ability to understand and read others' emotions plays a key role in enhancing one's social skills.

Understanding Emotions

Teenagers who experienced trauma quite often find it difficult to read social cues correctly. Guessing can lead to difficulties as they may jump to the wrong conclusion due to their reactivity systems being affected by their trauma. This can result in their having the most extreme reactions, which often culminates in the dysregulation of their emotions and actions. These emotions could be anger, frustration, distress and even aggression.

Here are some ways to help teenagers gain a better understanding of social cues and situations. Start out by showing how emotions are tied to facial expressions and body language: Watch TV and/or look at pictures in books, and point out facial expressions and body postures. Explain to them how the facial expression, body language and emotions are tied together. Then, create ways for your teenagers to practise so that they can develop a deeper understanding. You can even make it fun by doing 'people watching' when outside. The aim is to identify sad, angry and happy faces on the people in your vicinity. Another option is to undertake this activity while looking at pictures in books and magazines and/or on TV. I would also recommend seeking opportunities to name their and others' emotions as and when appropriate. For example, you can say, 'I can see that you are happy for you are smiling and laughing' or 'Your friend is frowning. I wonder how he is feeling'. The ability to understand social cues and situations will help your teenager strengthen their friendships and social interactions.

Developing Social Skills and the Ability to Handle Strong Feelings

Teenagers are often very emotional beings due to their brain development, as explained earlier in the book. This means that there will be many disappointments, fall outs with friends and hurt feelings. Teaching your teenagers how to handle disappointment will help them navigate the ups and downs of friendships. Teenagers with trauma find this extremely challenging for it is already hard for them to regulate their emotions. All you can do is offer a listening ear and be empathetic and nurturing. When appropriate, try to put their feelings into context, but do not invalidate how they feel. A word of warning: Never try to choose your teenagers' friends; you cannot control their friendships. Keep your opinions about their friends to yourself. What you can do is talk about what a friendship should be like and how it should be beneficial for both parties. Explain that the best type of friendship is one that allows them to speak openly and honestly without the fear of being judged. Friendships depend on listening as well as sharing. However, it does take time to make a good friend, and forming such a friendship requires one to put in the necessary time and effort. Explain to them that the more activities they participate in, the more likely it is that they will find new people to form friendships with. I think that it is important to offer them support in accessing other activity groups. They are likely to find this difficult and challenging. Anything that can get them out of their bedroom and off social media can only be of benefit. Moreover, it is also important to let them know that not all friendships last forever. People change as they mature and have other experiences, and this often leads to changes in their friendship groups. Discuss with them what qualities they would like in a friend and what qualities they would want a friend to see in them.

Praise When Appropriate

I advise you to praise your teenagers every time you see an improvement in their social skills and/or notice them reacting positively to a situation. Remember not to overpraise for this can set them up for failure. What is important is acknowledging how they behaved and asking them how they feel about it. Giving them the space to talk about it will help enhance their growth. You should not overpraise them because they might feel shame if they do not react in the way you would have liked the next time they face a similar situation. You do not want them to feel that you have too high expectations from them. All of the above are for trying to create new pathways in their brain so that they can develop their social interactions skills.

Dealing with Peer Pressure

I am sure that as parents and from experience you understand how peer pressure can force your teenagers to make poor choices. The choices can involve risky behaviour such as drug use, unsafe sexual behaviour and unsafe driving. Teenagers who struggle to make friends due to their trauma often undertake risky behaviour to seek positive affirmations and acceptance from their peers. Obviously, this will depend on the kind of friends they make for a large number of young people encourage their friends to do good. This is often referred to as positive peer pressure. However, I have already mentioned that teenagers affected by trauma have a very small pool of individuals to choose from when making friends, which quite often results in them socialising with young people who have problems of their own. You can try and explain the power of peer pressure to your teenagers so that they will, hopefully, make more informed choices. You must get them to see that friends can influence them in both positive and negative ways.

Modelling Behaviour

One of the best ways to teach your teenagers how to interact with others in a positive way is to model appropriate behaviour. You can also share with them your own experiences as a teenager and how you had to learn the necessary skills. Explain to them that it is okay to get it wrong; what is important is that they keep learning from their mistakes and continue trying to develop their social skills. Do set time aside to teach and practise with your teenagers for it helps, even if it just entails a simple activity like asking them to guess how you are feeling as you act out some cues at the dinner table. Be conscious of how you interact with your friends and family members in front of your teenagers for this can also be a good source of learning for them.

Conclusion

Hopefully, you can see that you can try several interventions to support teenagers with developmental trauma in navigating friendships. Yes, I am sure that at times they will make some bad choices, but I also know that a large majority of us have done the same and survived. All you can try and do is support them in developing their social skills and help them learn and accept their and others' emotions. There are many helpful activities that you can undertake to teach them about social cues. Positive modelling does help, and spending time to listen to their worries and reassure them is definitely time well spent. I would advise you to never say anything disapproving about their friendships, but you can approach this matter from a different angle by exploring with them what a 'good friend' is like. If they are isolating themselves and socialising only via social media, do be patient and encourage them to socialise in a face-to-face setting. This may mean being the resident taxi driver and/or having their friends over, but friendships are so important in all aspects of life, especially in one's teenage years. What is most important is that we never forget that it is their trauma that is making it challenging for them. It is not that they want to be 'antisocial' or are trying to make others unhappy or angry; they just do not know how to be 'appropriately social'. By teaching them social skills, you can help them create new, positive experiences that will help them in the present and future.

Therapeutically Parenting Teenagers with Developmental Trauma

Chapter 13:
EDUCATION

The majority of the therapeutic parents I meet often cringe when the subject of school comes into the conversation. A large number of these parents often share with me that their children have a terrible time at school. Some schools are better than others at supporting children and young people living with trauma on a daily basis. However, you may be required to travel a long distance, well out of your school catchment area, to access such schools. I have observed that over the last few years, schools have gained a better understanding of ACEs and that this does have an impact on the children and young people who attend them. However, there is still a long way to go. In England, looked-after children are more likely to be excluded from school and acquire lower grades than their peers in their year. This can often be attributed to the trauma they face due to previously experienced abuse and neglect. Their inability to regulate their emotions and experiences with toxic stress negatively affect their learning (Bombèr, 2007).

Lynn Miles (2019) captures the exact issues that need to be addressed in schools in her article 'Supporting young people who have had adverse childhood experiences'. She reflects on her own time at school and acknowledges that she was fortunate that a number of perceptive teachers at her school understood the need to intervene in a different way to deal with her anxiety and permanent hypervigilance. In the article, she shares how difficult it can be for pupils who live in constant fear each time they walk through the school gate. She argues that schools can assist in making life better for these children and young people by not only supporting them in achieving academically but also helping them heal. She identifies the need for an environment that instead of ignoring their suffering, allows them to learn, flourish and reach their full potential. Miles gives a comprehensive list of tools that can make a significant difference for children and young people with ACEs, and I have included the list below. I personally feel that her article and Louise Bombèr's (2007) excellent book *Inside I'm Hurting* grasp all the nuances of the school debate, and I cannot recommend them enough; both are definitely worth a read. I would personally recommend both to the head teacher and the lead for looked-after children at the school your teenager attends.

The following tools can have a significant impact in schools. I have copied them directly from Miles's (2019) article:

- Continuously maintain an awareness of the impact of ACEs, toxic stress and trauma, and strive to ensure that all pupils feel safe, supported and connected.
- Maintain a safe, predictable, calm environment that prioritises relationships and consistency.
- Show unconditional positive regard to all pupils (and school staff) at all times.
- Remember that behaviour is a symptom of the problem, not the problem. Be curious about behaviour – ask 'What happened to you?' rather than 'What is wrong with you?'.
- Eliminate stress triggers from the environment – loud voices, abrupt sounds, etc.
- Take an interest in the pupils – they need to know you care.
- Teach pupils to self-regulate and calm their stress response system.

- Listen to the pupils more and talk at them less.
- Focus on the positive – communicate pupils' successes to them and their families regularly.
- Support the pupils' caregivers and connect with the whole family – it improves the pupils' outcomes.
- Follow your instincts – welcome them back after a break.
- Take care of yourself – the children need you to be at your best.
- Do not take things personally – it is not about you.

Miles acknowledges that the processes of implementing these changes and attaining success with these pupils will be slow and challenging, but the evidence is clear: If we continue as we are, many vulnerable children will likely struggle for the rest of their lives.

Now, I think it will be advantageous to explore what you can do to support your teenagers throughout their education.

Finding the Right School

Prior to even considering any school, you might find it worthwhile to spend some time analysing how your teenagers' trauma impacts their behaviour. In a sense, you are undertaking a review of what you know and have observed while supporting your teenager. Here is a list of some of the issues you may want to reflect on:

- Can they sit still for long periods of time?
- How do they function in big groups?
- How do they respond to rules, and what is the likelihood that they will break said rules?
- How will they cope with having to move from class to class? What impact will this have on their anxiety?
- Will they be able to cope with a change of teacher several times per day?
- What are their organisational skills like?

- Will they be able to undress and dress themselves when participating in their physical education lessons?
- Will there be days when they refuse to go to school? What are their potential reasons for doing so?
- Will they have to come out of school to attend regular appointments?

This review will give you enough information for when you actually start to visit schools. Prior to this, I recommend undertaking some research about the schools in your local areas and further afield if necessary. A good starting point for your research is a phone call to the local authority who is responsible for the care order for your teenager. They should be able to put you in touch with the virtual school. The virtual school acts as a local authority champion to promote progress and educational attainment of children and young people who are or have been in care so that they achieve educational outcomes comparable to their peers' (Virtual School Kent [VSK], 2020). It will hopefully supply you with a list of schools that have a good record for supporting looked-after children and young people. If your teenager does not come under the local authority of the area where you live, the virtual school that is responsible for them will be able to liaise with the local authority of your area on your behalf. I also recommend reading Ofsted reports for specific schools and focusing on the schools' capacity to nurture pupils. Once you have found a school that interests you, ask your adoption or fostering agency if any of their carers send children and/or young people to that school. If yes, leave your number with them and ask them to enquire if the carer(s) could call you to share their views of the school in confidence. Wherever possible, seek such reviews from parents who are in a similar position as you for they will have a direct insight into how knowledgeable the school's staff is and how it responds to children and young people with developmental trauma.

Visiting Schools

Once armed with your shortlist of schools, it will be beneficial for you to visit each one in person. Each school must have a designated teacher for looked-after and previously looked-after children (Department for Education [DFE], 2018); their role entails taking the lead on the children's personal education plans (PEP), making sure that all their needs are met and supporting other members of staff in achieving outcomes for the children. I would highly recommend meeting with this teacher or at least ensuring that they will be present at the meeting when you attend the school.

Once you walk into a school, try and get a sense of the atmosphere. I would recommend arriving a little early for your meeting. Make sure to read their Ofsted report and visit their school website beforehand. What does the school say about its behavioural policies? How rigid are the policies? Yes, a teenager with developmental trauma does require clear boundaries and structure. However, some schools take this to the extremes. For example, they may stipulate

Therapeutically Parenting Teenagers with Developmental Trauma

the design and material of young people's hair bobbles or the actual measurement of their school socks. I cannot help but ask myself how these factors contribute to children and young people's educational achievements. Personally, I feel that this is more about controlling students rather than establishing boundaries and structures that support their educational attainment.

Once in the meeting, you can use the findings from the review you undertook regarding how your teenager responds in certain situations to enquire how the school would address their needs. What would their response be to specific behaviours? The meeting should give you an insight into the school's understanding of the impacts of ACEs and how aware they are about trauma-informed behaviours. I also recommend asking about the structures they have in place to work alongside the whole family and what communication channels they use. The type of experience your teenager has at school will definitely have an impact on the family/home, and vice versa, so this aspect is incredibly important.

Once you have chosen a school and your teenagers have been accepted, you need to discuss a transition plan. This should involve them visiting the school a good number of times, meeting with their teachers and spending some quality time with the designated teacher for looked-after children and young people. The designated teachers in particular are going to play an important role in ensuring that your teenager successfully attends secondary school. Hopefully, they will be trusted adults that your teenagers can build attachments with. They will undertake a role similar to yours – they will be the ones looking out for your teenager at school. They should have a good understanding of trauma-informed responses for this will be key in helping your teenager self-regulate as and when required. The visits might be a little overwhelming for your teenager, so I suggest that you take some pictures to look at when you both return home. The time leading up to your teenager actually starting their new school is really important for it can be used to explore their anxieties and how you can work together to overcome them. Share your own experiences, but do not minimise their feelings and anxieties. Most importantly, they should know that you have got their back and that you will do everything humanly possible to support them.

Parental Support of Teenagers Navigating the School System

In her article, Miles (2019) identified that it is highly likely that there will be some very kind, caring, sympathetic teachers who will be really accepting of your teenager. They are more than likely to be naturally empathetic and nurturing. They could be from any of the disciplines within the school curriculum. The designated teacher for looked-after young people and a number of support staff will also be available, forming a part of the team around your teenager. This team is crucial, and you need to have regular contact with the members who will form the support bubble for your child. You are also a very important member of this team. I would even say that, at times, you need to be the linchpin that holds the team together.

Communication Channels

Setting up a clear route of communication that involves all members of the team will be beneficial to you and the school and, more importantly, offer the support that your teenager will require. When things are not going well at home and/or if you are aware of certain trigger points, I would highly recommend informing all team members. Examples of trigger points could be the death anniversary of a birth family member, or the anniversary of the day your teenager became part of the care system. If something that happened at home and/or school has dysregulated your teenager, the school needs to be made aware of it. The same responsibility applies to the school. However, I am sure that you will receive regular calls, even daily sometimes. I would like to suggest here that rather than both parties making calls only in the event of challenging behaviour, it will be beneficial to also call or email each other when something goes exceptionally well. This can reduce the level of frustration that all members of the team may experience at certain times. Frustration about having to start from the same ground every day without a breakthrough can and often does contribute to compassion fatigue, which is explored in the next section of the book.

Timetable

Ensure that you have a copy of your teenager's timetable for you should be able to identify the lessons and/or teaching staff your teenager might be struggling with. You can then discuss with all the team members and devise a strategy to alleviate the anxiety and triggers. Moreover, you can discuss these issues at home and support your teenagers by being an empathetic listener. You may also have to offer support in preparing for the next school day by ensuring that they have all the necessary equipment and materials in their school bags. I would recommend taking it one day at a time, enjoying the good times when everything is going well and trying to have a 'matter-of-fact' attitude when it is not. Remember, school is only one part of your teenager's day; do not let it overtake all the precious family time you spend together in the evenings and on weekends.

Homework

Homework can become a point of contention between you and your child. I would suggest offering as much support as you can but not at the peril of making the home a battleground each evening. Home, and preferably school, should be a place where the teenager in your care feels safe and receives lots of empathy and nurturing. Try to ensure that the school explores alternatives to handing out punishments when your teenager is not able to complete homework. This is where the team can be most effective.

Sensitive Issues

Ensure you have open discussions with the designated teacher for looked-after children regarding the curriculum, especially around personal, social, health and economic (PSHE) education. This area of the curriculum does cover many sensitive issues such as abuse, drug use and domestic violence. For many young people, this will be both educational and informative. Your teenager must already be aware of it, and it is highly likely that he or she has lived through it and was a recipient of the abuse. The pain and anguish this may bring to the fore for your teenager in a class of thirty will be unbearable. I think Donovan (2019) covers this really well when she explains how the fallout from such lessons may happen either at school or in the home. She emphasises that these are the risks that our teenagers have been exposed to in real life, not only in theory.

Education, Health and Care Plan (EHC Plan)

An EHC plan is for children and young people aged up to twenty-five years who need more support than is available through special educational support. EHC plans identify educational, health and social needs and set up additional support to meet these needs (DFE, 2014). I would argue that every child who has experienced ACEs that resulted in developmental trauma is eligible for an EHC plan. This point should be raised at the personal education plan (PEP) meetings. All the members of the team around your young person and the virtual school should be involved in getting a plan in place for your teenager. This, for me, is a passport to education that comes with all the support teenagers need, and it is reviewed on an annual basis. The plan will stay with them till they are twenty-five years old. This is a fantastic resource with numerous benefits, both social and financial.

Therapeutically Parenting Teenagers with Developmental Trauma

Conclusion

Education is a very important element of everyone's life. I remember reading somewhere that our school years can be the best or worst years of our lives. Many of us can look back with satisfaction and remember the teacher who went the extra mile for us as well as the friendships we made, lost and still have to this day. Unfortunately, for many teenagers with developmental trauma, their school experience is an immensely negative one. Schools are improving, but they still have a long way to go. Miles's (2019) article and Bombèr's (2007) book summarise the school debate perfectly and put forward some excellent proposals for both schools and therapeutic parents. As therapeutic parents, you have a professional and personal responsibility to enable your teenagers to participate in the education system. As outlined in this chapter, you can help them in a number of ways. Without doubt, it is a lot more profitable and enjoyable to work alongside schools than against them. A number of teenagers with developmental trauma cannot navigate a large secondary school, and they may have to opt for alternative provisions. All of the above suggestions still apply because a place being signposted as 'alternative provision' does not automatically mean that it is ideal for your teenager. Further, I think that it is important to ask for an assessment to see if your teenager is eligible for an EHC plan. This plan is so important because it provides the extra support they need educationally, socially and emotionally. Yes, school is important, but you must always remember that you are supporting teenagers who have to cope with trauma on a regular basis. School will throw so many challenges at them, and you must ensure that they feel that home is a safe place they can retreat to. School is school, and home is home. Ideally, both will become safe havens for your teenagers, and you need to make sure that no matter what happens at school, you never continue or pursue it when your teenagers get home. Yes, be supportive, let them vent, and help them self-regulate. Then, brush yourself down, and get ready for the next day.

TAKING CARE OF YOURSELF

Chapter 14:
COMPASSION FATIGUE AND SELF-CARE

Compassion fatigue is a condition characterised by emotional and physical exhaustion that lead to a diminished capacity to empathise with or feel compassion for others; this is often described as the negative cost of caring. It is when the carer feels drained due to the child's behaviours and needs. Consequently, the brain undergoes physiological changes, leaving the carer incapable of connecting with the child or teenager. It is sometimes mistakenly referred to as secondary traumatic stress. Secondary trauma means that the carer actually feels traumatised by the child's experiences. Examples of this could be reliving the young person's experiences in your dreams and feeling angry about what has happened to them.

In a research undertaken by the Bristol University with a sample of foster carers, it was found that seventy-five percent of them showed signs of compassion fatigue and burnout, which is higher than the numbers for carers in other professions. Bearing in mind that foster carers often receive more support than adopters and carers do on other orders such as special guardianship order (SGO), this is a major concern (Naish, 2018).

A part of compassion fatigue is often referred to as burnout. It refers to when carers feel isolated and unattached emotionally and deploy a strategy of just getting through each day. This leaves them with the capacity to meet only the most basic needs of the children. A study showed that carers also feel isolated because they reported that social workers do not really understand how hard it is to look after a child with developmental trauma. They also felt that there was a blame culture and revealed that some professionals actually judge them and accuse them of not fulfilling their roles (Ottaway & Selwyn, 2016).

Caring for children and young people who experienced abuse, neglect, trauma, separation and loss is a demanding and highly stressful occupation. The role requires carers to have good mental health and wellbeing for they will have complex demands placed on them by those in their care. Carers who care for traumatised children and young people are at a high risk of compassion fatigue due to the complexity of their role. Their homes are also their place of work, so the opportunities to have a break are minimal. This affects not only their mental health and wellbeing but also the consistency of the care they provide.

Red Flags

We all have our own red flags, and everyone's flags are different. When they are triggered, they send you soaring to your emotional highs. Anyone else who is in close proximity will wonder what is wrong for what was said or took place may seem very minor to them. Red flags are an individual thing because they are woven into who you are as a person. For example, you may become very frustrated and agitated when people arrive late, disrupting your well-made plans. Quite often, red flags are based on past experiences and can even be triggers related to bad memories. When you are feeling drained and on the verge of exhaustion, you are obviously more prone to having your red flags activated.

Many people go through life without undergoing the red flag experience. However, this is not the case with those caring for teenagers with developmental trauma, and I can guarantee that you will face your red flags head on! The teenagers in your care will try to identify your red flags and then go full out to trigger them to see what you are made of. This enables them to control the emotional environment of the home. I explored this in Chapter 11 when discussing family life. I acknowledged that some teenagers will find it extremely difficult to adapt to and settle into a calm family environment. Therefore, they will do their utmost to recreate the environment they are used to, an environment full of hostility and tension.

Dealing with red flags is not an easy task for they are a deep-rooted part of you. A good exercise is to take some time out to identify your red flags. What are the little things that really annoy you and make your emotions go totally out of control? Once you have identified them, you will initially feel that what you can do about them is limited. However, acknowledging them is actually a part of accepting them. You and your parenting partner can talk to each other about your respective red flags. Awareness of each other's red flags will allow you both to step in and offer support to the other as and when necessary. In a sense, you operate as a 'tag team'. If you are a single parent, I would suggest sharing your red flags with a member from your support bubble so that someone else is aware of them and can help you if the need arises (Donovan, 2019). The question of whether you should share them with the whole family was elegantly addressed by Donovan; she likened sharing your red flags to handing out the codes for nuclear warheads. This is a decision for you to make based on how well you know your teenager.

Identifying your red flags and acknowledging that you are more vulnerable when tired and exhausted, in part, answers the question of how to avoid overreacting when your red flags are triggered. Further, I think that you need to be asking yourself what you can do or put in place to avoid compassion fatigue. The best way to avoid burnout is to identify the need for healthy, meaningful self-care. Before engaging in self-care, you have to recognise the need for and benefits of it. I would argue that if you cannot take care of your own mental wellbeing, you cannot expect to be capable of providing twenty-four-hour emotional support seven days a week to the teenagers in your care. They need you to be at the top of your game.

Self-Care

Without healthy, meaningful self-care, you will be functioning on near empty or, even worse, at a deficit; either can lead to burnout. This will result in constant arguments at home, leaving you feeling inadequate as a therapeutic parent. When you are functioning on empty, you have nothing or very little to give. You cannot pour from an empty cup. Your teenager will still have the same needs and exhibit the same challenging behaviours. What will be different though is your tolerance level. What you do in such a situation will make all the difference, not only for you but also for the teenager in your care.

Before exploring healthy, meaningful self-care it will be beneficial to discuss some of the obstacles that prevent carers from refreshing and reequipping themselves.

Quite often, when raising the issue of self-care with carers, I hear the phrase, 'I don't have time for that'. They thrust their phone or diary at me and show me numerous scheduled meetings and a long to-do list. They then dismiss the idea of undertaking any self-care activities for they do not even know when they will find the time to do the week's shopping. Another phrase I often hear is, 'I can't leave the kids; they need me right now'. Carers tend to be very generous with their time, and once they commit themselves to caring for a child, they will not go back on it. My experience is that many carers are terrible at putting themselves first; it is just not in their nature. They constantly talk themselves out of finding time for themselves. They even feel guilty just for thinking about it. You often hear carers say, 'We never take a respite because it is not fair to the children'. I do worry when I hear statements like these and often wonder if the children in their care might appreciate a break themselves.

When experiencing compassion fatigue or on the verge of it, it is very difficult to know what you need to do to return to your previous self. You feel physically drained, muddle brained and emotionally fragile. Any and all suggestions that require some preparation seem daunting, and you lack the self-motivation to start the process. The idea of self-care sounds wonderful but out of reach.

To avoid finding yourself in the above situation, you need to prioritise self-care even when you feel at the top of your game. Meaningful self-care is what keeps you feeling capable of confronting any of the challenges that you come across on a regular basis. Self-care needs to be an integral part of your therapeutic parenting.

Sarah Naish (2018) summarised self-care poignantly, pointing out that it is not self-indulgent, selfish or even reckless to engage in self-care; support and respite should be a part of your daily, weekly and monthly routine. It is a fundamental necessity and requirement for therapeutic parents in particular – self-care prevents compassion fatigue and ensures that the children and young people in your care receive consistent, empathetic, nurturing care. Most importantly, self-care prevents disruption and further trauma for all concerned. Naish (2018) argued that the foundations of therapeutic parenting rely on empathetic, skilled support and self-care.

Engaging in self-care is crucial, but the choice of activities is down to personal preference and what you find really rewarding and relaxing. Some carers might want to go rock climbing or walk ten miles; others, like me, will want to spend a few hours crown green bowling. Like I said, it is down to individual choice. Below is a list of some potential self-care activities, but it is important that you make your own list and then start planning them into your busy schedule.

Ideas for Self-care

- Put an hour aside to chat with your friend on the phone.
- Go for a walk.
- Have a long bath.
- Go swimming.
- Meet friends for lunch.
- Go to the cinema with a friend or partner.
- Treat yourself to a cup of coffee with cake and quiet.
- Read a book in the garden.

- Attend a support group.
- Join a local club, for example, the table tennis or karate clubs or the operatic society.
- Go fishing.
- Sit and meditate.
- Book a short holiday.

Conclusion

Managing the impact of exposure to the trauma of others requires a daily, continuous commitment to your own self-care. When time is short and needs are great, you often ignore your own needs because you are too focused on others. Carving out some quality time for yourself might be challenging and may take a lot of planning. However, this is a very important ingredient in therapeutic parenting – you need to constantly refuel and replenish your own energy bank. Your weekly schedule must contain some time for you to relax, think, reflect and maintain your connections with others for the benefit of your own wellbeing. Maintaining balance in your life does prevent you from becoming drained and exhausted. Making and honouring this commitment to yourself enables you to protect your attunement and direct your empathy towards your traumatised teenager.

Chapter 15:

WORKING WITH OTHER PROFESSIONALS

Having a child become a part of your family has many benefits, but their trauma-led behaviours do create challenges. They will have a number of other professionals in their lives, all of whom are responsible for their wellbeing. These will more than likely include social workers, health workers, educational specialists, teachers, therapists, independent reviewing officers, councillors and support workers. You will have the responsibility of not only taking care of the child but also of working alongside all these professionals. This chapter explores some of the things that you may want to take into consideration when working as a part of a team to support your child.

Many social work teams subscribe to the philosophy of relationship-based practice when working in a partnership. Relationship-based practice is more a state of mind than a theory; it is a way of communicating and building and strengthening relationships, which then help resolve existing difficulties. Communication is key to developing these relationships, and it is an essential ingredient for making any intervention effective. In relationship-based practice, social or emotional problems are subjected to integrated or psychosocial approaches rather than technical or clinical responses. Therefore, relationships are a network for support, help and repair (Glasgow, 2018). I personally feel that relationship-based practice is really important and even more effective when underpinned by emotional intelligence, especially when working in a team.

I explored emotional intelligence in Chapter 8 as a means of retraining your subconscious mind as well as improving your skills as a therapeutic parent. It also plays a key role when you are working with other professionals. Remember, there are five key components of emotional intelligence: self-awareness, self-regulation, motivation, social skills and empathy (Goleman, 1998).

As said earlier, when working with other professionals to care for a teenager with developmental trauma, you will be a part of a team. I am sure that you are already aware that not everyone will agree with you all the time and that many professionals will be from different disciplines and have their own philosophies and culture.

Employing a relationship-based practice approach helps develop positive relationships, which, in turn, facilitate open and honest discussions. Hopefully, this will resolve any differences that arise when dealing with difficult situations and prioritising interventions. Communication will be key to developing professional relationships within the team, which will ultimately lead to positive outcomes for the teenager in your care. Underpinning this approach with emotional intelligence will make the team more effective. Emotionally intelligent people know that although emotions can be powerful, they are temporary. When a highly charged emotional discussion happens with regard to your teenager, the emotionally intelligent response would be to take some time to regulate your emotions before putting your point across. This will allow everyone involved to calm down and think more rationally about all the factors surrounding the disagreement.

The benefits of using your emotional intelligence when working with other professionals are outlined below:

Greater Self-Awareness

Emotionally intelligent people are good at not only thinking about how other people might feel but also understanding their own feelings. Self-awareness allows people to consider the many different factors that contribute to their emotions. Being aware of your emotions will enable you to regulate them and act appropriately.

Empathy for Others

A considerable part of emotional intelligence is the ability to think about and empathise with how other people are feeling. This often involves considering how you would respond if you were in the same situation. You do this on a daily basis with the teenagers in your care, so it is good to utilise this skill in other environments as well. People who have strong emotional intelligence are able to consider the perspectives, experiences and emotions of others. This is an excellent skill to have when working with other professionals, and it will facilitate the processes of problem solving and decision-making.

How to Use Emotional Intelligence

Emotional intelligence is essential for good interpersonal communication. Some experts believe that this ability is more important in determining life success than IQ alone. Fortunately, there are things that you can do to strengthen your own social and emotional intelligence (Goleman, 1998). Having good emotional intelligence skills means being a good listener and having the ability to understand what others are communicating both verbally and non-verbally. If you are emotionally intelligent, you will also be able to read others' body language, which carries a great deal of meaning. When you sense that someone is feeling a certain way, you will be able to consider the different factors that might be contributing to their emotion. The ability to reason with emotions is an important part of emotional intelligence. You will be able to consider how your own emotions are influencing your decisions and behaviours. Similarly, when others are talking, you will be able to assess what influence their emotions are having on what they are trying to communicate. Understanding emotions is the key to better relationships, improved wellbeing and stronger communication skills. Emotional intelligence can be used in many different ways in your daily life. Some ways to practise emotional intelligence when working as a part of the team include the following:

- Accepting criticism and responsibility
- Moving on after making a mistake
- Saying 'no' when you need to
- Sharing your feelings with others
- Solving problems in ways that work for everyone
- Having empathy for other people
- Having great listening skills
- Knowing why you do the things you do
- Not being judgemental of others

Therapeutically Parenting Teenagers with Developmental Trauma

Conclusion

Your emotional intelligence skills will be extremely useful when you are part of a team that cares for your teenager; you can apply these skills when advocating on their behalf. You will find that you will be able to quickly gain the trust of other professionals. Without doubt, emotional intelligence is an amazing skill to acquire and apply in team situations. Your input will be valued as you value the input from others. Emotional intelligence will also equip you with the tools needed to deal with change, and others will follow your lead. Moreover, you will be able to handle tough conversations by emotionally connecting with the others on the team to find a resolution. All this will make others see you as a person they can trust and as a valued asset to the team.

Chapter 16:

THE CORE PRINCIPLES OF THERAPEUTIC PARENTING

Below are short summaries of each chapter in this book. You can use these as a quick reference guide. You may also find it useful to read through them periodically to maintain your focus, continue your mind training and stay motivated.

SECTION 1: PARENTING

Chapter 1: Why Our Teenagers Act the Way They Do

A large amount of well-documented research has shown that a child who experienced neglect and abuse is likely to develop significant behavioural and emotional problems due to which they will not be able to make secure attachments. Children and teenagers who face adverse childhood experiences (ACEs) usually go on to develop trauma. They are said to have 'developmental trauma' for the trauma does have a significant impact on their brain development.

The chapter discusses how the brain undergoes some fundamental changes when young people reach adolescence. Teenagers who experienced trauma need to not only adapt to these typical changes but also deal with the developmental effects of past abuse and neglect. Trauma and adolescence work together to interfere with teenagers' sense of self and how they think others see them. When a child experiences repetitive trauma, the brain develops certain behaviours for survival. This affects how the teenager acts socially, emotionally and cognitively. A number of trauma-informed behaviours are explored in detail in this chapter. These include hypervigilance, emotional regulation, empathy, trust, shame and guilt, control issues and the internal working model.

Chapter 2: Why Standardised Parenting is Not the Answer

The four most popular styles of 'standardised' parenting are authoritarian, authoritative, permissive and uninvolved parenting. This chapter explores all four styles in the context of parenting teenagers with secure or insecure attachments. Teenagers with insecure attachments are often referred to as having developmental trauma.

Studies have shown that securely attached teenagers can derive many benefits from the authoritative parenting style and that they will more than likely thrive if parented by this approach. However, for teenagers with developmental trauma, all four parenting styles are problematic. All these standard styles, some more than others, are likely to cause fear and evoke more shame. The studies used to explore each parenting style have certain limitations: The links between the parenting styles and behaviour are based on research on the connection between two or more people, but this cannot establish definitive cause-and-effect relationships. Other variables also need to be taken into consideration: Culture, teenagers' temperament, their perceptions of parental treatment and social influences also play an important role in determining teenagers' behaviours.

Then, what approach should be employed to parent teenagers with developmental trauma? Since they have to deal with adolescence-induced changes as well as the developmental effects of past abuse and neglect, they require a parenting style that is trauma-informed and that will make them feel safe and secure. The therapeutic parenting style meets both these needs.

Chapter 3: Therapeutic Parenting

A mini literature review of therapeutic parenting is presented in this chapter with the conclusion that therapeutic parenting focuses on making the teenager feel secure and safe. This style of parenting has high structure underpinned with nurture. It sees behaviour as a method of communication. It is all about trying to connect with the teenager's feelings, emotions, fears, anxieties and traumatic memories. This is done by employing playfulness, acceptance, curiosity and empathy (PACE). Therapeutic parents need to be resolute about what they are doing and know why they are using a specific tool or strategy. Being a therapeutic parent is an intentional choice. This means having a plan in place to make it easier for you to respond to your child and not merely react to behaviours. This style of parenting is effective, but it can take an exceptionally long time for the strategies to have an impact. Therapeutic parenting is very demanding for the parent and immensely time-consuming.

SECTION 2: TRAINING YOURSELF TO BE A THERAPEUTIC PARENT

Chapter 4: Mind Training

The brain regulates not only your physical self but also what happens mentally. Your mind relentlessly filters and brings to your attention information and stimuli that confirm your pre-existing beliefs; it also presents before you repeated thoughts and impulses that imitate and mirror what you have previously experienced. Therefore, it is important for you to recognise the role of your subconscious mind when trying to transition from one parenting style to another; if the subconscious is left unchecked, it will keep reverting you to your pre-existing parental experiences and previous responses. Therefore, in this chapter, I identify the need and recognise the importance of reprogramming your subconscious mind. I focus on the role of self-doubt and the impact it can have when you are trying to bring changes in your subconscious mind. Tackling self-doubt is an important aspect of mind training. Self-doubt can lead to stress and anxiety, which trigger your fight-or-flight reflex. In this chapter, I explore strategies for dealing with self-doubt and emphasise that rather than dealing with it in isolation, it would be more effective to tackle self-doubt through approaches such as goal setting, affirmations and creative visualisation. My argument is that you can retrain your subconscious mind to act the way you want it to in certain situations by practising regular affirmations coupled with creative visualisation. You need your subconscious mind to filter challenging behaviours and routinely seek out therapeutic responses that are informed by the underlying methods and strategies of therapeutic parenting.

Chapter 5: Goal Setting

In this chapter, I acknowledge that goal setting is an especially important component of mind training. Setting goals triggers new behaviours, guides your focus and sustains progression. Goals not only align your focus but also promote self-mastery, in this case, of therapeutic parenting. Realistically, you cannot manage what you cannot measure, and you cannot improve upon something that you do not effectively manage. Setting goals does enable you to achieve this and more. The idea of reviewing your current parenting style is discussed and put forward as a good strategy for identifying your initial goals. Goals should be specific, measurable, achievable, realistic and time-bound. You will need one long-term goal that is underpinned by a number of intermediate goals and a series of short-term goals, all of which should be displayed on a goal chart that you can see every day. Through SMART goals, you can monitor and track your progress as a therapeutic parent.

Therapeutically Parenting Teenagers with Developmental Trauma

Chapter 6: Affirmations

Affirmations are specific positive suggestions that you repeat to yourself with the intention of achieving your goals, building your self-confidence and maintaining your motivation.

The process and benefits of using positive affirmations are explored in detail in this Chapter. Regularly employing this process can change your mindset and enable your brain to actually take the affirmations as facts. The guidelines for undertaking affirmations are also detailed in this chapter: Your affirmations must be positive, stated in the present tense and declared out loud with conviction. The change will not happen overnight for it can take anywhere from 25 to 30 days of constant programming for it to become a part of your mental programme. Affirmations generally work as a tool for shifting your mindset and achieving your goals, but they are not a magic injection for instant success. You have a role to play in ensuring that the change happens. Most importantly, once you have changed your mindset, you need to act. Repeating an affirmation can boost your motivation and confidence, but you still have to take some action yourself. The theory here is that if you keep telling yourself that you can do something, before long, it will become a part of your subconscious. The impact of this on your confidence will be astounding.

Chapter 7: Creative Visualisation

This chapter outlines how visualisation is the norm for those wishing to excel in almost all areas of sport. Visualisation techniques are also used alongside other traditional medical procedures to enhance healing. Through creative visualisation, you can reprogramme your subconscious mind to act in a therapeutic way rather than based on your previous experiences. All you need to do is supply your brain with information about appropriate therapeutic parenting strategies over a sustained period of time.

This chapter explores the process of visualisation and gives examples related to working with a teenager with developmental trauma. The aim is to embed into your subconscious mind the vision of you dealing with a challenging situation and responding therapeutically. Then, you must try to retain these images for you need to play them over and over again in your mind. This is in preparation for your encounter with this or similar situations in real life.

I also detail how your brain operates on autopilot, enabling you to perform tasks quickly, accurately and without conscious effort. Autopilot mode seems to be run by a set of brain structures called the default mode network (DMN). When the brain is in this mode, it is actually assessing past events and planning for the future. It enters a state of consciousness. Evidence has shown that your responses become faster and more accurate in this mode.

Further, goal setting, affirmations and visualisation are all important methods of retraining your subconscious mind. Creative visualisation is a really powerful tool when combined with affirmations.

Chapter 8: Emotional Intelligence

Emotional intelligence involves understanding and managing emotions. While the ability to express and control emotions is essential, so is the ability to understand, interpret and respond to the emotions of others. Daniel Goleman identified five components of emotional intelligence: self-awareness, self-regulation, internal motivation, empathy and social skills

Self-awareness is the capability of being aware of different aspects of yourself, such as your behaviours, feelings, emotions and characteristics. Recognising and understanding our emotions are essential emotional intelligence skills. It is necessary to not only recognise our emotions but also understand the effects of our emotions, actions and moods on others. This means that you should be able to name emotions clearly and concisely.

Self-regulation refers to regulating and managing your emotions. This does not mean locking down your emotions or blocking them out. On the contrary, self-regulation is about expressing your emotions appropriately.

Internal motivation initiates, guides and maintains an individual's goal-oriented behaviours. It is responsible for why you act in certain ways, whether it is going to the fridge to get some food to ease your hunger or reading a book to gain knowledge. Motivation is driven by biological, emotional, social and cognitive forces that activate one's behaviour. Often referred to as 'self-motivation', it is used to explain why an individual engages in certain behaviours. You can actually say that motivation is the driver of all human actions.

Empathy is another indispensable component of emotional intelligence. Teenagers who experienced trauma find it exceedingly difficult to show empathy for they probably did not have many opportunities to learn it from adults. Due to their past ACEs, they must have shut down their own feelings as a way of coping. This does affect their ability to develop the skill of empathy. Exploring the application of Dan Hughes's PACE model, I explain that by showing empathy, we can let our teenagers know that we feel compassion for them and that we want to try and understand how they are feeling. By being empathetic, we can actively show them that their inner emotions, feelings and experiences are of utmost importance to us.

Empathy, or the ability to understand how others are feeling, is an absolutely critical qualify of emotional intelligence. It involves more than just being able to recognise the emotional states of others – empathy is the ability to emotionally understand how others are feeling, see things from their point of view and imagine oneself in their place.

Social skills, i.e. being able to interact and engage well with others, form another important aspect of emotional intelligence. Having strong social skills allows individuals to build meaningful relationships with other people while developing a stronger understanding of themselves and others.

A considerable part of emotional intelligence is the ability to think about and empathise with how other people are feeling. This often involves considering how you would respond if you were in the same situation. Knowing what motivates you to become a therapeutic parent is the start of the journey. Being socially intelligent will boost your interactions in a wide range of settings and your relationship with the teenager in your care. People who have high emotional intelligence are able to consider the perspectives, experiences and emotions of other people and use this information to explain why people behave the way they do. This enables them to think and respond therapeutically.

SECTION 3: PARENTING YOUR TEENAGER

Chapter 9: Communicating With Teenagers With Developmental Trauma

The most important element of therapeutic parenting is the relationship that you have or are trying to develop with the teenager in your care. This is crucial if you are going to undertake any therapeutic work with them. Initiating some banter with them will help build an initial relationship that the teenager will, hopefully, invest in. A positive family environment is really important for children and young people who experienced trauma; they need to live in a safe and nurturing home, one that allows them to experience mutual enjoyment, respect and opportunities.

While establishing a relationship, it is important to strike a balance between the banter and seriousness. Doing this is not easy and will take considerable effort on your part.

Therapeutically Parenting Teenagers with Developmental Trauma

You need to be able to read the non-verbal cues of your teenager for this is crucial if you are to connect with them emotionally. Finally, creating an empathetic and nurturing environment will enable you to connect with your teenager, which will, in turn, lead to emotional attunement.

Chapter 10: Developing Resilience in Your Teenager

This chapter outlines how each and every one of us responds differently when faced with stressful situations. Resilience is often defined as the ability to respond positively and learn from stressful situations. To build resilience, children and teenagers need access to a series of protective factors. Research has shown that children and teenagers who had secure attachments that led to positive internal working models have all the protective factors that contribute towards the building of resilience. However, teenagers with disorganised internal working models, which make them feel worthless and/or undeserving of positive experiences, find it difficult to build resilience because struggling to manage relationships, feelings and/ or past experiences does have a major impact on the development of resilience.

The presence of protective factors, particularly safe, stable and nurturing relationships, can often alleviate the consequences of ACEs. Individuals, families and communities can all influence the development of many protective factors throughout a teenager's life, which can affect their development.

The following protective factors are identified in the chapter as means of helping your teenager build resilience: a close relationship with an adult in a family unit, parent resilience, caregiver's knowledge and application of positive parenting skills, identifying and cultivating a sense of purpose through the development of individual factors and social connections. You have a key role to play in each one of the protective factors.

Building resilience takes time; but without the necessary protective factors, it is unlikely to happen. Through therapeutic parenting, you can not only support your teenager through their trauma but, more importantly, also play a major role in helping them go on to live with the ability to reach their full potential.

Chapter 11: Family Life

A core component in the creation of a calm family atmosphere is your own ability to self-regulate. Being emotionally intelligent will help you be aware of your own and your family members' emotions.

Clear boundaries and structures will facilitate consistency. As the teenagers start adapting to the boundaries and structures, you can expect to see a reduction in their challenging behaviours. Being in a family atmosphere where they experience empathy and nurturing will help them explore feelings of trust and wellbeing.

This chapter also recognises that creating the family atmosphere before the teenagers join your family is relatively easy, but maintaining this is challenging. What you need to take into consideration is that the teenagers are leaving a totally different environment, one that was very chaotic and that forced them to learn how to live with fear and constant disruption. Therefore, they will find it exceedingly difficult to settle in an atmosphere that is totally alien to them. Do not be surprised if they try to recreate the atmosphere they are used to.

Opening up your family to a new family member will always lead to challenges. What is important is to learn and move forward together. This will be a new experience for you all because a new member will change the family dynamic. However, creating a fun-filled, empathetic environment where all family members are nurtured will make the journey so much easier.

A number of helpful pointers are given in the chapter. Some additional factors are also explored: holidays, your relationship, the need to therapeutically parent together, how certain dates can be triggers and not being too hard on yourself for you are only human.

Chapter 12: Friendships

Friendships are incredibly important during adolescence. Teenage friendships help young people feel a sense of acceptance and belonging. They are key to developing their compassion, empathy and caring. Friendships may be problematic, but they are beneficial because they help teenagers develop a sense of identity outside the family. A host of social skills are required to develop and maintain friendships. These are complex, and they do take time to learn. For children and young people who experienced trauma, learning social skills can be extremely challenging. Trauma has a serious impact on their normal developmental processes, making it difficult for them to understand social cues, develop good emotional regulation, adopt the perspective of others and develop empathy.

Thus, they are often unable to develop and/or maintain friendships, so they usually make poor friendship choices. This can and usually does involve them participating in risk-taking behaviours. Traumatised teenagers can quickly go through numerous short-term friendships, thereby experiencing a lot of hurt and rejection. This confirms their internal working model that they are not good enough to have friends. As a result, they may turn to the Internet and social media for developing friendships. This chapter discusses a large number of factors related to social media, its potential to lead to isolation and a host of safeguarding issues.

I also explore a number of ways in which you can help your teenager develop friendships, such as building on their existing social skills, enabling them to understand their and others' emotions and helping them simultaneously develop social skills and the ability to handle big disappointments, which are a part of adolescent friendships. This chapter also sheds light on positive and negative peer pressure, and finally, it highlights the need to offer praise and model your own behaviour when helping your teenager develop and maintain friendships.

Chapter 13: Education

Some schools are better than others when it comes to supporting teenagers living with developmental trauma due to ACEs. You may have to travel outside your catchment area to find a forward-thinking school with regard to trauma-informed practice. Things are improving, but there is still a long way to go. Lynn Miles and Louise Bombèr have shared some excellent ideas on supporting children and young people with ACEs within the education system.

Before finding a school, it is recommended that you take some time to analyse how your teenager's trauma affects his or her behaviour; in a sense, you are reviewing what you know and have observed while supporting your teenager. Once armed with the findings of your review, make a shortlist of schools and arrange to visit them. Ensure that the dedicated teacher for looked-after young people is present at the meeting for he or she will be the key support person for your teenager. The findings from your review will enable you to ask specific behaviour-related questions to find out what behavioural response each school would apply.

Once your teenager is accepted for admission to the school, make sure that you have a transition plan in place to make the move to the new school as smooth as possible. Communication is fundamental, so you need to set up a two-way communication system with the school by involving all the members of staff who will be part of the team responsible for your teenager. Another thing you may want to give some thought to is pre-empting triggers by focusing on their timetable, homework and curriculum to check if there are sensitive issues related to your teenager's ACEs. Additionally, consider applying for an education, health and care (EHC) plan as it can be immensely beneficial for children living with trauma on a daily basis.

Finally, this chapter elaborates on the need to separate school issues from home. Yes, school is important, but you must always remember that you are supporting teenagers who have to regularly cope with trauma. School will throw many challenges at them, and you must ensure that they feel that home is a safe place.

SECTION FOUR: TAKING CARE OF YOURSELF

Chapter 14: Compassion Fatigue and Self-Care

Compassion fatigue is a condition characterised by emotional and physical exhaustion that lead to a diminished ability to empathise or feel compassion for others. This is often described as the negative cost of caring. Compassion fatigue is also frequently referred to as burnout. This is when carers feel isolated and unattached emotionally and just resolve to try and get through each day. This leaves them with the capacity to meet only the most basic needs of the children in their care.

Caring for children who have experienced abuse, neglect, trauma, separation and loss is a demanding and highly stressful occupation. Carers need to have good mental health and wellbeing to be able to handle the complex demands placed on them by those in their care. Carers who care for traumatised children are at high risk of compassion fatigue due to the complexity of their role. Their home is also their place of work, so the opportunities to have a break are minimal.

This chapter also focuses on red flags, which are different for every person. What is common for all is that when these flags are triggered, we are sent soaring to our emotional heights within a matter of seconds. Red flags are woven into who you are as a person. Quite often, they are based on past experiences and can even be triggers related to bad memories. You are more prone to having your red flags triggered when you feel drained and on the verge of exhaustion.

Self-care is very important for without it, you are likely to find yourself functioning on near empty or, even worse, at a deficit, which can lead to burnout. This will lead to constant arguments in the home, which will leave you feeling inadequate as a therapeutic parent. When you are functioning on empty, you have nothing or very little to give. You cannot pour from an empty cup.

Sarah Naish summarised self-care poignantly, pointing out that it is not self-indulgent, selfish or reckless to engage in self-care; support and respite should be part of your daily, weekly or monthly routine. Self-care prevents compassion fatigue and ensures that the children and young people in your care receive consistent, empathetic, nurturing care.

Self-care is a personal thing for we have different interests and like to socialise in different ways. A list of self-care activities is also provided in this chapter.

Maintaining balance in your life prevents you from becoming drained and exhausted. Making and honouring this commitment to yourself enables you to attune to and empathise with your traumatised teenager.

Chapter 15: Working With Other Professionals

Having a child become part of your family has many benefits, but their trauma-led behaviours do create challenges. However, you can rely on a number of other professionals to take up the responsibility for the child's wellbeing.

Relationship-based practice is often used in the field of social work when working in a partnership. It is more a state of mind than a theory; it is a way of communicating

Therapeutically Parenting Teenagers with Developmental Trauma

and building and strengthening relationships, which then help resolve existing difficulties. Communication is the key to developing these relationships, and it is an essential ingredient that makes interventions effective, enabling you to secure positive outcomes for the teenager in your care. Combining a relationship-based practice with emotional intelligence will increase the effectiveness of the team caring for your teenager. Emotionally intelligent people know that emotions are powerful but temporary.

In this chapter, I detail the application of emotional intelligence in the context of working with others and acknowledge the need for greater self-awareness and empathy. Examples depicting how to utilise emotional intelligence when working with other professionals are presented. In short, emotional intelligence will equip you with the tools required to deal with change; as a result, others will follow your lead. You will be able to handle tough conversations by emotionally connecting with the others on the team to find a resolution. This will make others see you as a trustworthy person and a valued asset.

ACKNOWLEDGMENTS

I would like to say a big thank you to all the young people who I have had the pleasure of working alongside over the past three decades. I am also extremely grateful for all the encouragement and support I receive from my family and friends and colleagues.

When writing this book, I came to realise how many of my life experiences have informed my parenting philosophy. Therefore, I think it is only right to thank everyone who has played a part in my life, albeit socially or work related.

I would also like to give a special mention to all the young people who have become part of our family. Thank you for making it such a 'richer' experience and such a rewarding environment.

References

Chapter 1

Bowlby, J. (1998). *A secure base: Clinical applications of attachment theory*. Routledge.

Center on the Developing Child at Harvard University. (2018). *What are ACEs?* https://developingchild.harvard.edu/resources/aces-and-toxic-stress-frequently-asked-questions/

Golding, K. (2008). *Nurturing attachments: Supporting children who are fostered or adopted*. Jessica Kingsley Publishers.

Hughes, D. (2012). *Parenting a child with emotional and behavioural difficulties*. CoramBAAF.

Libertin, A. (2019). *The teen years: Brain development and trauma recovery*. NACAC. https://www.nacac.org/resource/the-teen-years-brain-development-and-trauma-recovery/

Watson, P. (2018). *What is developmental trauma/ACEs?* https://www.porticonetwork.ca/web/childhood-trauma-toolkit/developmental-trauma

Chapter 2

Baumrind, D. (1967). Child care practices anteceding three patterns of preschool behavior. *Genetic Psychology Monographs, 75*(1), 43–83.

Maccoby, E., & Martin, J. (1983). Socialization in the context of the family: Parent-child interaction. In *Handbook of child psychology: Socialization, personality, and social development* (Vol. 4, pp. 1–101).

Chapter 3

Attachment Trauma Network. (2020). *Therapeutic parenting.* https://www.attachmenttraumanetwork.org/parenting/

Bombèr, L. (2007). *Inside I'm hurting.* Worth Publishing.

Cairns, K. (2015). *Attachment, trauma and resilience.* BAAF.

Golding, K. (2008). *Nurturing attachments.* Jessica Kingsley Publishers.

Golding, K., & Hughes, D. (2012). *Creating loving attachments.* Jessica Kingsley Publishers.

Hughes, D. (2012). *Parenting a child with emotional and behavioural difficulties.* CoramBAAF.

Hughes, D., & Baylin, J. (2012). *Brain-based parenting.* W. W. Norton and Company Limited.

Hughes, D. (2016). *Parenting a child with trauma.* CoramBAAF.

Naish, S. (2016). *Therapeutic parenting in a nutshell.* Amazon.

Naish, S. (2018). *The A to Z of therapeutic parenting: Strategies and solutions.* Jessica Kingsley Publishers.

Naish, S., & Dillon, S. (2020). *The quick guide to therapeutic parenting.* Jessica Kingsley Publishers.

Nelson, J., & Lott, L. (2012). *Positive discipline for teenagers.* Three Rivers Press.

Siegel, D. (2012). *The whole-brain child.* Robinson.

Siegel, D. (2017). *Brainstorm.* Scribe.

Chapter 4

Fleming, A. (2020). *The Inner Game of Crown Green Bowling.* KDP Amazon.

Lorrison, G. (2014). *Visualisation*. CreateSpace Independent Publishing.

Morrison, M. (2014). *Goal setting: 10 Easy steps to keep motivated and master your personal goals*. CreateSpace Independent Publishing.

Siegel, D. (2012). *The whole-brain child*. Robinson.

Chapter 6

Davis, T. (2019). *Positive Affirmations: 11 Keys to Affirmations That Work*. Psychology Today. https://www.psychologytoday.com/gb/blog/click-here-happiness/201901/positive-affirmations-11-keys-affirmations-work

Lim, S. (2020). *5 Simple Rules How to Make Your Affirmations Work*. Stunning Motivation. https://stunningmotivation.com/how-to-make-affirmations-work/

Lively, K. (2014). *Affirmation: The Why, What, How, and What If?* Psychology Today. https://www.psychologytoday.com/gb/blog/smart-relationships/201403/affirmations-the-why-what-how-and-what-iif

Chapter 7

Buckner, RL (2015). *Know Your Brain: Default Mode Network*. https://www.neuroscientificallychallenged.com/blog/know-your-brain-default-mode-network

Davenport, S. (2018). *Visualisation: Recovery and the Power of the mind*. https://www.reboothealth.co.uk/blog/visualisation-hospital-operation

Chapter 8

Carpenter, D. (2020). *How to develop empathy in your relationships*. https://www.verywellmind.com/how-you-can-practice-self-regulation

Cuncic, A. (2020). *How to develop and practice self-regulation*. https://www.verywellmind.com/how-you-can-practice-self-regulation

Dweck, C. (2017). *Mindset – Changing the way you think to fulfil your full potential* (6th ed.). Robinson.

Goleman, D. (2020). *Emotional intelligence: Why it can matter more than IQ*. Bloomsbury Publishing.

Goleman, D. (1998). *Working with emotional intelligence*. Bantam.

Hockenbury, D., & Hockenbury, S. E. (2007). *Discovering psychology*. Worth Publishers.

Kendra, C. (2021). *5 key emotional intelligence skills.* https://www.verywellmind.com/components-of-emotional-intelligence

Loftus, E. F. (1988). *Memory: Surprising new insights into how we remember and why we forget*. Rowman & Littlefield Publishers.

Scott, E. (2020). *How to become more mindful in your everyday life*. https://www.verywellmind.com/mindfulness-exercises-for-everyday-life

Tull, M. (2020). *What is distress tolerance*. https://www.verywellmind.com/distress-tolerance

Chapter 9

Golding, K. (2008). *Nurturing attachments*. Jessica Kingsley Publishers.

Holland, J. (2020). *How do I get my teenager to talk to me?* https://www.relate.org.uk/blog/2015/3/12/how-do-i-get-my-teenager-talk-me

Siegel, D. (2012). *The whole-brain child*. Robinson.

Chapter 10

Moore, C. (2020). *Resilience theory: What research articles in psychology teach us*. https://positivepsychology.com/resilience-theory/

Therapeutically Parenting Teenagers with Developmental Trauma

Chapter 11

Donovan, S. (2019). *The unofficial guide to therapeutic parenting – The teen years.* Jessica Kingsley Publishers.

Golding, K. (2008). *Nurturing attachments: Supporting children who are fostered or adopted.* Jessica Kingsley Publishers.

Chapter 12

Fenkel, C. (2017). *The link between smartphone addiction and social isolation in teens.* https://health.usnews.com/health-care/for-better/articles/2017-10-11/the-power-of-an-irl-community-creating-space-for-teens-to-unplug-and-engage

Pantic, I. (2014). *Online social networking and mental health.* https://www.ncbi.nlm.nih.gov/pmc/articles/PMC4183915/

Siegel, D. (2017). *Brainstorm.* Scribe.

Underwood, M. (2015). Being 13: Social media and the hidden world of young adolescents. https://www.documentcloud.org/documents/2448422-being-13-report.html

Chapter 13

Bombèr, L. (2007). *Inside I'm hurting.* Worth Publishing.

DFE. (2014). *Thematic report: The education, health and care (EHC) planning pathway for families that are new to the SEN system.* https://assets.publishing.service.gov.uk/government/uploads/system/uploads/attachment_data/file/275104/RR326B_EHC_planning_pathway_-_FINAL.pdf

DFE. (2018). *Statutory guidance: Designated teacher for looked-after and previously looked-after children.* https://www.gov.uk/government/publications/designated-teacher-for-looked-after-children

Donovan, S. (2019). *The unofficial guide to therapeutic parenting – The teen years*. Jessica Kingsley Publishers.

Miles, L. (2019). *Supporting children who have had adverse childhood experiences*. https://www.headteacher-update.com/best-practice-article/adverse-childhood-experiences-and-the-implications-for-schools/215017/

VSK. (2020). *What is a virtual school*? https://www.virtualschool.lea.kent.sch.uk/about-vsk/what-is-a-virtual-school#:~:text=The%20Virtual%20School%20acts%20as,outcomes%20comparable%20to%20their%20peers

Chapter 14

Donovan, S. (2019). *The unofficial guide to therapeutic parenting – The teen years*. Jessica Kingsley Publishers.

Naish, S. (2018). *The A to Z of therapeutic parenting: Strategies and solutions*. Jessica Kingsley Publishers.

Ottaway, H., & Selwyn, J. (2016). *No one told us it would be like this: Compassion fatigue and foster care*. The Hadley Centre, University of Bristol.

Chapter 15

Glasgow, M. (2018). *Relationship based practice: What does it really look like?* https://www.staf.scot/relationship-based-practice-what-does-it-really-look-like?

Goleman, D. (1998). *Working with emotional intelligence*. Bantam.

Printed in Great Britain
by Amazon